Jeremy Torz and Steven Macatonia, founders of Union Han[...] been a driving force in the UK coffee-scene since the mid-[...] the country's first boutique micro-roastery. They were behind the successful growth of the UK's first quality-focused coffee bar chain, and in recent years the two coffee-obsessed proprietors have developed an industry-leading platform for sustainable sourcing of premium quality coffees direct from farmers and producers around the world. Union Hand-Roasted Coffee supplies some of the finest restaurants, cutting edge cafés and retailers around the UK and direct from their roastery through unionroasted.com to enthusiastic coffee drinkers at home.

Recent awards for Union Hand-Roasted Coffee include: The Queen's Award for Enterprise: Sustainable Development 2017, Allegra European Coffee Awards: 2016, 2015 and 2014 Best Artisan Coffee Roaster (Europe); 2015 Most Ethical Coffee Company; 2015 Outstanding contribution to the coffee industry: Jeremy Torz; and 29 Great Taste Awards 2013–16.

REAL FRESH
COFFEE

REAL FRESH
COFFEE

HOW TO SOURCE, ROAST, GRIND AND
BREW YOUR OWN PERFECT CUP

JEREMY TORZ & STEVEN MACATONIA

PAVILION

CONTENTS

INTRODUCTION

People often ask a question that we find impossible to answer: 'How do I find *the* coffee that's right for me?' For us, coffee is always about a willingness to explore. If you take the view that our tastes and preferences may depend upon mood, time of day, or what else we happen to be eating or drinking at the time – and you buy into the view that coffees can and do taste different – we don't think that any single country, continent, farm or blend can offer a single answer. It's an approach that we rarely take in other food or drink choices – after all, do you only ever buy one type or style of wine? Do you only eat one kind of food, whether Italian or Turkish or Vietnamese? Didn't think so. So why narrow the focus when you're dealing with coffee?

Recent years have seen amazing changes in our food culture. Street-food operators reflect their global origins – Nordic, Korean, Peruvian, Mexican, Jamaican – with authenticity and passion. But while a small but growing number of gastronauts are exploring lots of strange new worlds, most coffee drinkers still see coffee as little more than a functional food – something to wake them up or boost energy levels. The darker, stronger and more bitter the brew, the better! Many people's love of coffee, particularly espresso, seems rooted in the love of a caffeine kick, usually wrapped in a thick, luxurious towel of textured milk.

Having come into the world of coffee roasting purely out of interest in how it tastes, we have made it our passion to explore and to taste objectively, to seek out the differences and to share them with our customers. It's not always an easy task. The poor quality of most mass-market coffee has resulted in low expectations and lack of interest.

But a revolution has occurred at all levels in the industry. While speciality coffee still represents only a tiny percentage of world trade, it has an increasingly loud voice. The movement arguably began in the mid-1990s around San Francisco and Seattle on the west coast of the USA. Against a backdrop of declining coffee consumption through the 1970s and 1980s, the new wave of speciality coffee grew by presenting something new and exciting to coffee drinkers. During the four years we spent living in the States in the early- to mid-1990s, we started to discover small-batch, locally roasted coffees that were a real cut above what we'd been drinking at home in London.

Having seen that these brews seemed so superior, we had to find out what made this true and why. We started to apply some scientific methodology, an approach that became a working practice throughout our learning journey, and one that makes sense to anyone who has ever built, tested or tried to perfect any skill or invention: change *one thing at a time* and try to understand the results.

To do this, we'd set out to buy coffees from one country, which could reasonably be assumed to be similar to each other, in a range of roasts from light to dark. By tasting them, we began to understand one aspect of the coffee picture: the effect of roasting. Then we tried coffees from one company, but from different countries, with a similar level of roast, to start getting an idea of how geography affects taste. From there we had the absolute basics. Over the years, we have come to see how complicated (and fascinating) the spectrum of coffee flavours can be.

The multinational coffee industry – with its huge advertising budgets and 'dumbed down' messages – has produced a narrow vocabulary. Many coffee drinkers describe coffee using only four words: strong, mild, bitter and smooth. Yet when we are tasting in our cupping room at Union's roastery, it can sound more like a vineyard tasting room, with references to fruits, nuts, chocolate and so many more descriptors.

There are hundreds of ways to describe coffee's different aromas and flavours, which depend upon where it was grown, how it was processed from tree to bean, how it was roasted and ultimately brewed.

When we start to understand the different choices we can make, we can begin to make selections that appeal to our moods and preferences and explore with an open mind. Then it's possible to truly enjoy the differences in coffee just as we do with wine, malt whisky or craft beer.

So, how to answer the question, 'how do I find the coffee that's right for me?' Our advice is: treat it as an unfolding journey of increasing pleasure and reward. When it comes to 'the right coffee' there is more than one correct answer.

One of the things in our coffee lives that we continue to love after over 20 years in business is seeing that lightbulb moment when someone 'just gets coffee'. We can both bring to mind a coffee that we have really enjoyed and feel our taste buds tingling, and the thought of someone else experiencing that joy and recognition excites us. Perhaps coffee is our religion. If it is, we are certainly not the only members. At small, independent coffee bars and shops, coffee lovers are saying that what's in the cup is more important than what's around it. In addition to the familiar espresso-based options, cafés are increasingly offering single-cup brews of high-quality single-estate coffees, brewed in a variety of seemingly fiddly gadgets designed to showcase the flavour of the coffee. This trend, referred to as the 'third wave of coffee', has expanded the coffee experience. At Union, we are proud to be part of this wave.

The ultimate beanbag: Jeremy and Steven (left and right) sitting on top of the (coffee) world at their roastery in East London.

Jeremy Torz and Steven Macatonia
London, 2016

COFFEE ORIGINS

When you look at your breakfast cup of coffee and breathe in its gorgeous aromas, you're at the final stage – delightful for you – of an incredibly complicated process. A 'simple' agricultural product has found its way through many hands and many thousands of miles before becoming the drink you enjoy so much. Your enjoyment depends, first of all, on the variety or varieties of coffee grown on the farm where your beans came from. It depends on where those farms are located, and how they are run, and by whom. It depends on the way the beans were processed at (or near) the farm where they were grown. All these factors have a profound effect on the character of the coffee in your cup.

And this is all before the final crucial points in the production of your cup – roasting and brewing – which you'll read about later in this book. Sounds complicated? Well, it is. But if you focus only on one aspect of this story, focus on the farmers. Without them, there would be nothing to drink. They are the starting point of a complex economy – and one that, without appropriate support, can leave a less-than-pleasant taste in the mouths of those on whom the whole industry depends.

COFFEE GROWING

As coffee roasters, we depend on the farmers whom we source from to produce coffee beans with the most exciting potential. Roasting the beans is a transformative process, but it can only draw out and balance the various characteristics already within the bean: we cannot make silk purses out of sows' ears!

Many factors influence the level of quality and development of flavour characteristics in the coffee bean, from the climate, altitude, type of soil and the species and variety of coffee tree through to the harvesting and processing of the ripe beans.

Climate and microclimate

All coffee originated from East Africa, around Ethiopia and Sudan, and as such it remains a broadly tropical plant with a penchant for hotter climes. It's not a case of the hotter the better, however: both of the main species grown for coffee today (Arabica and Robusta) have a range of temperatures in which they thrive – too hot and the plants can be weakened, resulting in reduced production and making them more susceptible to pests and diseases. At the other extreme, coffee is not frost-tolerant: very low temperatures can cause the total loss of a crop. The regions in which we find coffee growing today are not by accident of nature: it has been planted for commercial production in regions where climate and conditions suit the tree of either species.

For Arabica, the preferred species for drinkers of quality coffee, the ideal temperature range is between 15 and 24°C (60 and 75°F) and for the best coffee the trees need warm days with good sun (to allow sugars to develop inside the fruit), combined with cool nights. These optimum conditions usually occur in the tropical band around the Equator, between 23° North and 23° South.

Rainfall is also an important element. Arabica requires around 1500–2500mm (60–100 inches) of rain distributed over

a period of nine months. The first rains trigger the flowering. Rain is needed throughout the growing season as the fruit (known as coffee cherries) develops, but there then needs to be a dry season during the three months of the year when the cherries are harvested and dried.

A few countries, such as Colombia and Kenya, have widely distributed rainfall patterns, giving them two crops a year, which are referred to as the main and fly crops (in Colombia the latter is known as the *mitaca* crop). Generally the best quality is obtained from the main crop.

Coffee requires light soils that have a good gravel or stony content so that the plant remains well drained and cool. The ideal soil is slightly acidic, with a pH of around 5 to 7 and good levels of nitrogen, phosphorous and potassium. In many growing countries, depending mostly on latitude and the intensity of the sun while the fruit is maturing, the coffee plant may require dappled shade to protect the young cherries from scorching before they are ripe. This shade is normally provided by indigenous trees planted by the coffee farmer.

Altitude

In general, higher-altitude coffees have superior flavour. This is because while coffee trees thrive in tropical zones, the higher the temperature (within limits), the more vigorously the plant grows and the greater the quantity of fruit. Anyone who has grown herbs knows that in strong sun and warm conditions the plants tend to 'bolt' or put on large volumes of leaf. On tasting, however, this bounty is often found to be lacking in flavour: it's as if the flavour has become diluted through the greater leaf quantity. In cooler conditions, the plants don't grow so vigorously, but the slower growth seems to become focused into better flavours. Coffee trees are similar. In very warm conditions, they produce lots of fast-growing and fast-maturing fruit with lower sugar content and reduced quality when ripe. In mountainous and high-altitude regions, generally around 1200–2000m (4000–6500ft) above sea level, it remains cooler than in lower regions. The trees produce less growth and fruit, and the fruit matures more slowly and yields denser beans which concentrate the sugars, organic acids and other compounds that create the clear flavour profiles found in quality coffee.

But higher altitudes also often mean steeper hills and more difficult management of coffee fields. The finest coffees are hand-picked, and higher elevations also require producers to put extra effort into implementing farm management practices that avoid soil erosion.

Coffee growing in the mountains, Chirripó National Park region, Costa Rica. Steep terraces like these can produce outstanding coffee, but farming here is a formidable challenge – and an expensive one.

ELEVATION: THE QUALITY DIFFERENCE

Arabica, the cool customer
Has a lower yield • Higher sugar content
Less resistant to disease • Likes lower
temperatures • Bigger beans
More antioxidants

- → 900m (3000ft) above sea level

Robusta, some like it hotter
Has high yield • Higher caffeine content
High resistance to disease • Likes higher
temperatures • Smaller beans
Requires greater rainfall • Fewer antioxidants

MEXICO

CUBA
JAMAICA
GUATEMALA HONDURAS
EL SALVADOR NICARAGUA
COSTA RICA PANAMA

COLOMBIA

PERU BRAZIL

IVORY COAST

ETHIOPIA
KENYA
UGANDA
RWANDA
BURUNDI
TANZANIA

● Robusta

● Robusta and Arabica

● Arabica

TOP COFFEE-EXPORTING COUNTRIES

Country	60kg bags
1 Brazil	45,342,000
2 Vietnam	27,500,000
3 Colombia	11,600,000
4 Indonesia	6,850,000
5 Ethiopia	6,500,000
6 India	5,005,000
7 Mexico	4,500,000
8 Guatemala	4,000,000
9 Peru	3,500,000
10 Honduras	2,700,000
11 Uganda	2,500,000
12 Ivory Coast	2,350,000
13 Costa Rica	1,808,000
14 El Salvador	1,374,000
15 Nicaragua	1,300,000
16 Papua New Guinea	1,125,000
19 Tanzania	917,000
21 Kenya	850,000
26 Burundi	481,000
29 Rwanda	350,000
31 Cuba	225,000
37 Panama	75,000
42 Jamaica	35,000

NOTE World export figures are quoted in 60kg bags; countries that produce in larger bags are adjusted to 60kg equivalent. African countries and Brazil export in 60kg bags. Central and South America (apart from Brazil) ship in 69kg bags – with the exception of Colombia, which ships in 70kg bags.

(2014 figures. Courtesy International Coffee Organization. Countries omitted from the above list are not commonly available to consumers in international markets and are mainly used anonymously in commercial blends.)

COFFEE AND CLIMATE CHANGE

You may have your own views on the chatter and science reported around the matter of climate change, and who or what is responsible for it. Our view is shaped by meeting with coffee farmers out in the vast expanses of countryside around the world, and that experience suggests there can be no doubt that something is changing.

We've had many conversations with younger coffee farmers and often ask, 'compared to your father's time, how different are things today?' We used to expect to hear comments about learning new growing or processing methods, and better access to information and markets. Now the most common thing we hear is how much harder it is today because of the weather.

Arabica coffee has a very narrow tolerance for temperature and rainfall. Rain needs to come at particular times of the year, during flowering and cherry development and not after the harvest period when farmers are trying to dry the crop. Temperatures elevated above the ideal stress coffee plants in various ways and often make them more susceptible to pests and diseases.

Our story-based 'evidence' has more recently been backed up by a collaboration in Ethiopia that we are undertaking with the coffee science team at the Royal Botanic Gardens, Kew, one of the world's most experienced and respected plant research organizations. In 2012, Dr Aaron Davis and his team completed a computer modelling analysis that projected a reduction in land suitable for wild Arabica coffee forests in the region of between 85 per cent and 99.7 per cent by as soon as 2080. Areas that had traditionally been perfectly suited to Arabica coffee were identified as becoming increasingly unsuitable throughout this century. As wild and cultivated Arabica coffee occurs in more or less the same places, this indicates a negative impact for coffee farming, too. While it's certainly the case that this could simply mean a relocation of coffee from lower to higher regions, the logistic and human elements of such an undertaking

are not straightforward. The Kew team and Ethiopian collaborators are now looking at this issue in much more detail and with a specific focus on how to ensure resilience for Ethiopia's 15 million coffee farmers.

For now, governments are looking at where certain farming activities are conducted and some communities are already being relocated to areas that have a more suitable climate. When transplanted, however, many villages take time to establish productive land and re-establish themselves.

Changes in rainfall patterns cause problems for farmers who traditionally dry their coffee on tables or patios after harvest. Mechanical coffee dryers are increasingly used to overcome this but they increase costs for producers.

A shallow gene pool

While there are numerous cultivars of *Coffea arabica* coffee grown commercially today, they mostly originate from a handful of seed introductions. Over the generations, breeding from within this small gene pool has further narrowed the genetic diversity. This happens with many cultivated crops, most famously the banana, whose most common cultivar (Cavendish) is balanced upon a knife edge, as it is losing its resistance to Panama disease, caused by a fungal pathogen.

Coffee has been cross-bred over the years to offer some resistance to common plant diseases, but in many cases this has not resulted in good quality, or flavours in the cup that are acceptable to consumers. But progress has been made, and there are now some that are showing increasing promise.

Coffee farmers' workshop, Yayu Forest Reserve, Ethiopia. At the front of the class (from left to right) Steven, Pascale Schuit and Dr Aaron Davis lead a discovery workshop for smallholders.

Coffee, trees and forests

One other major challenge to coffee and farming is the issue of deforestation. One of the main drivers here is population growth in the rural areas of developing countries. As infant mortality declines and health management improves, the need to grow food increasingly threatens natural forest areas as land is cleared for cultivation.

Loss of forest is not only a tragedy for the sake of global carbon capture opportunities, but almost invisibly it causes deterioration in local climate conditions through loss of shade and the 'cooling effects' of forest, and the loss of other 'ecosystem benefits', including soil preservation and watershed provision. As these areas are lost, so is the complex interplay of flora and fauna commonly known as biodiversity.

Since 2013, at Union Hand-Roasted, we've been part of a plan to work alongside the Plant Resources team at the Royal Botanic Gardens, Kew, with communities in the western highland region of Ethiopia around the Yayu Wild Forest Biosphere. Having lost over 70 per cent of its forests in the last century, Ethiopia has designated a protected forest to preserve one of its most important wild coffee resources. We have committed to a three-year plan to help farmers in five cooperatives farming within a 'transition zone' to improve the quality of their coffee. We are providing technical training, post-harvesting support and education to develop cupping skills so that they can better understand what they produce and hence attain a higher market value. Purchasing this coffee at sustainable prices gives them the opportunity to earn stable incomes, without having to convert the forest for other crops. The amazing and beautiful forest that they live in is part of their story and they are more than proud to look after it – as long as the forest provides them with an income. We feel that this is a great relationship based on the right reasons for developing coffee quality, and which provides a community with opportunity and a future based on a sustainable market relationship, rather than charity.

THE COFFEE TREE AND ITS FRUIT

Coffee trees are perennials. Once they have grown to maturity, they produce annual fruits referred to as cherries; at the centre of the fruit are the seeds, known as coffee beans. After depulping, washing and drying these become the raw 'green' coffee beans, ready for roasting and, ultimately, drinking.

Different varieties of coffee tree, grown in different soils and conditions, have slightly different flavour profiles. Usually, varieties are selected to suit the local soil conditions, with flavour characteristics often a secondary consideration. Nowadays, however, farmers producing for the speciality market increasingly view flavour as the primary factor and work to manage the trees within the local conditions.

Most coffee tree varieties will grow to a height of several metres, but are usually pruned to making picking easier. Dwarf varieties exist, and some have been bred specifically to confer resistance to pests or diseases or drought-like conditions.

All the flavours that we know and love in coffee arise from the sugars and other compounds that develop within the seed as it matures and ripens. Caffeine is present mainly in the fruit but also to a lesser degree in the leaves. It is thought that the bitter character of caffeine may act as a natural insect repellent. Today, we only drink the brew from the roasted bean, but in some parts of Africa and the Middle East, a tea-like brew sometimes known as *qahwa* (the origin of our word coffee) was made from the toasted leaves. In some areas this is still consumed today.

A woodcut made in Nuremberg in 1681 shows a healthy coffee tree in 'Mesopothamia' with a group of men (enjoying a cup?) relaxing in the background.

The life of a coffee tree

Coffee trees start their life in nurseries, where seeds from a prior season are planted into small pots and allowed to germinate, which normally takes around six to eight weeks. When it first germinates, the bean rises up out of the soil on top of the delicate stem. Gradually the first pair of leaves opens out from within and the bean falls away. At this stage, the plants are referred to as 'little soldiers'. They remain in their pots for around six to 12 months, during which time they are largely shaded to protect the delicate new growth. After this, the young shrubs are planted out into the field to begin their maturation to fruiting production, which takes around three to four years.

The longevity of a coffee tree depends in large part on the care and attention it is given during its productive life. Common practice is to prune the tree so as to develop three main stems, one of which is cut back each year on a rotating basis, always leaving two productive and one regenerative to help maintain decent yields. If managed well, trees can produce good crops for up to 15–20 years before replanting is needed. They can live much longer, however: up to around 100 years. But these old trees will not be commercially viable due to very low cherry production.

When rains stimulate flowering, dense white blossoms erupt from tiny buds which form in clusters around the base of each leaf and open as pure white, tiny flowers about 1cm (½ inch) across. The flowers are heavily scented of jasmine and it is common to see bees busily collecting the nectar, although coffee trees are self-pollinating and do not need the insect assistance. In some communities, beekeeping and honey have become an important second source of income for coffee producers: they can sell the honey at a time when the coffee crop is still some way from being ready to sell.

The flowers die back after around one or two weeks. From this point the small seed pods at their base develop and mature into coffee cherries over a nine-month period.

Top: Coffee seeds germinating to provide new seedlings.
Centre: Nursery area, with 'little soldiers' on the left and juvenile plants around 12 months old on the right.
Bottom: Mature coffee trees in full flower.

As the cherry grows, the two seeds inside it grow too. The outer fruit limits their space for growing, and this causes the inner surface of each seed to flatten as they are held against each other, forming the distinctive shape of the coffee bean. Occasionally, only one seed develops inside the cherry, and with no partner to hold it in shape, it forms a rounded bean. The Spanish word for a bean of this type is *caracol*, which means snail or seashell. In English we refer to them as 'peaberries', and they tend to make up around 5–10 per cent of a coffee crop. As some people believe that they have a different flavour character from the rest of the crop (some say sweeter, some say milder), they are usually mechanically separated from the rest of the crop after drying and can be sold for a price premium over 'regular' beans. Personally, we have never found a great deal of difference in the peaberry coffee from a well-managed farm that is already producing good coffee.

Coffee cherries turn from green to red as they ripen, although in some varieties the ripe fruit is yellow. The ripened colour does not confer any unique properties, but in the change from green to yellow it can be harder to quickly identify fully ripe yellow cherries. As a result, quality in the cup can be less consistent if processing is not very carefully managed.

Inside the coffee cherry

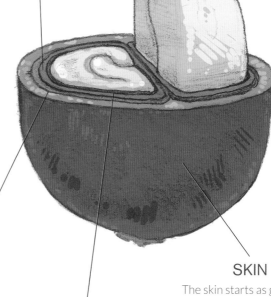

PARCHMENT

This is the protective paper-like covering around the two internal beans. During the drying process it acts like a parasol, protecting the beans from direct sunlight. It is removed during the husking and hulling process.

GREEN BEANS

Inside each cherry are two green beans. These are often compared to peanuts in the sense that they are two halves of a whole.

SKIN

The skin starts as green and develops to a rich red when ripe. It is thick and bitter, creating a great barrier against insects and disease.

MUCILAGE

This is the sticky fruit pulp. It is extremely sweet and has the texture of grapes. It is removed along with the skin and is often used as fertilizer.

SILVERSKIN/ COFFEE CHAFF

A very fine skin on the outside of the bean which disintegrates during the roasting process.

VARIETIES OF COFFEE

Chardonnay, Cabernet Sauvignon, Pinot Noir: these are all grape varieties that many of us have come to know, and we may have some understanding of the kinds of wine they produce. Yet many people are surprised that there are different varieties of coffee, even though it is understood that grapes, apples, oranges and garden flowers exist across a range of naturally occurring varieties and cultivars (cultivated varieties). Just as some flowers are crossed and hybridized to enhance particular aspects of flower colour or scent, coffee trees can be selectively bred to develop certain characteristics.

Above left: Typica varietal laden with maturing but as yet unripe coffee cherries. The cherries develop in clusters around each leaf node. Above right: Not all cherries turn red on ripening. Shown here is the Yellow Bourbon variety. Extra care must be taken when picking as complete colour change is less apparent than in red varieties.

Most of the varieties grown today come from a common ancestry, when *Coffea eugenioides* (one of four early species of the genus *Rubiaceae*) met with *Coffea canephora* to produce *Coffea arabica*. This is now widely believed to have occurred in Ethiopia, where the variety established itself. *Coffea arabica*, commonly known as Arabica, is the only kind this book is concerned with. (The other major species, *Coffea canephora*, commonly known as Robusta, is nowadays usually used only for lower quality blends or instant coffee.) As Arabica gradually spread around the world, it adapted. Through this natural adaptation, and as a result of plant breeding, new varieties developed that either suited different soil and climatic conditions or showed resilience to pests and plant diseases they encountered.

As plant science developed over the 20th century, new varieties were produced by the development and research organizations funded to greater or lesser degrees by national producer organizations and governments. Some, such as the legendary but unpoetically named SL-28 from Kenya, came about as a result of seeking drought- and rust-disease-resistant crops. Though aimed solely at solving a technical problem, the research project 'accidentally' yielded a variety with greater complexity.

Today there are more than 30 commonly found varieties of coffee in cultivation worldwide. From our own tasting and research we often prefer those we refer to as heritage or heirloom style. Two examples are Typica – from which all others arose – and Bourbon, Typica's first 'offspring' (more correctly, the first sustainable mutation). Though more challenging to grow and manage commercially, their flavour profiles are of outstanding quality.

Bourbon One of the first varieties to begin the worldwide colonization of coffee. In the early 18th century, a few Typica trees were taken by French merchants to the island of Bourbon (now Réunion) in the Indian Ocean. Once planted there they mutated to give a modified variety that has a higher yield and exceptional sweetness. Gentle milk-chocolate notes are often characteristic of the cup. Compared to modern varieties it has a relatively low yield and is more difficult to grow. Commonly grown in Brazil, Rwanda and El Salvador, the cherries mainly ripen to red, but ripe yellow fruit is often seen in Brazil.

Catuai A cross between Caturra and Mundo Novo, bred in Brazil in 1949. The tree is relatively compact, growing to an average height of 1.5m (5ft), with densely branched stems that give a high yield, and is relatively hardy, with some natural resistance to disease. Cup quality is generally recognized to be good. Widely planted in Central America, the variety comes in red and yellow forms.

Caturra This Bourbon mutation is a dwarf variety, popular because it can be harvested easily. A well-regarded variety for cup quality,

it can be grown over a wide range of altitudes, from around 1000m (3300ft) up to 2000m (6500ft), its acidity profile becoming really well developed at 1450m (4750ft) or higher.

Gesha Also known as Geisha, this is a direct descendant of an early Ethiopian variety that was relatively unrecognized until the early 2000s, when its star rose after the coffee was entered in a quality competition in Panama. Its previous history is subject to much debate, but it appears to have been collected as a specimen from Ethiopia and planted in a development and research plot in Costa Rica in the 1950s. Seeds were taken from Costa Rica to Panama by an enterprising grower and since its award-winning debut in that competition, many farmers in Central and South America have planted it because of the high prices its crop achieves. The high price is due to a genuinely different and delightful floral-aromatic cup as well as the challenge of growing the notoriously difficult plant with its very low yield. As more farmers grow it for its price, be careful: not all will give the care and attention that this variety needs and not all crops will have the same character as the competition lot that sparked the initial interest.

Mundo Novo Originating in and still mainly grown in Brazil, this is a cross between Typica and Bourbon that occurred naturally. Offering a higher yield than its parent plants, it maintains good cup quality at the lower altitudes commonly found in the coffee-growing regions of Brazil, around 800–1000m (2600–3300ft).

Pacas A natural mutation of Bourbon discovered in El Salvador and now grown in many Central American countries. Pacas remains popular due to high yields and a dense fruiting stem, producing sweet coffees often described as being similar to Bourbon but with a brighter acidity.

Pacamara Also a product of El Salvador, the Paca was crossed with the Maragogype, a tree with bold broad leaves and unusually large cherries that yield large beans. This remains true in the resulting Pacamara; its fruit offers coffees with rich chocolate undertones that in the best cases are balanced with bright floral-fruit and soft citrus notes.

SL-28 This has become a modern hero in Kenya. Originally created from selective breeding of a drought-resistant strain collected around

Tanganyika (now northern Tanzania) in the 1930s by a research station in Kenya, it can produce vibrant, full-bodied coffees with a bright blackcurrant flavour if managed carefully and grown at altitudes over 1250m (4100ft).

Typica The original coffee taken out from Ethiopia via Yemen and on to the rest of the world by Dutch traders throughout the 18th century. The Dutch East Indies (now Indonesia), especially Java and Sumatra, was the first place outside of Ethiopia and Arabia where coffee was widely cultivated. Typica spawned many other local varieties (Sumatra and Java types and also a Robusta-hybrid called Timor or Tim-Tim) that are still grown today. Typica coffees have excellent cup qualities and the variety is grown widely around the world.

SINGLE-VARIETY COFFEE

Many producers have a mixture of two or three coffee tree varieties on their plots. This helps to manage or mitigate loss through factors such as particular pests or diseases. In the case of more progressive farmers, growing a number of different varieties allows them to respond to specific variations in microclimate created by the altitude profile and sun availability on different facing slopes.

It is common practice for all of a farm's coffee to be harvested and processed together, with the resulting crop being characteristic of the farm or local region. As consumers get more information, however, they, along with roasters, are increasingly seeking out single-variety lots. Farmers who are able to manage their land well, and receive a price that compensates for this, can harvest and process each variety separately.

Sign marking a single varietal plot of Catuai at Finca (farm) Alaska in the Chirripó region, Costa Rica.

HARVEST

Harvesting coffee is the biggest annual operation undertaken on a coffee farm. Even seemingly large farms can operate with relatively few workers through the year, but at harvest the number swells tenfold. In places such as Central America it is common for coffee pickers to be migratory workers who follow the harvest season as it moves south. This transient workforce presents challenges for quality, because the picking can make the difference between a low-value commodity coffee and one destined for higher prices and more demanding markets.

Over a period of nine months, the coffee cherries mature and ripen, changing from a deep green colour to scarlet or 'cherry red'; within the fruit, sugars are developing – an invisible but essential indicator of ripeness. The challenge facing farmers and pickers is that on any given tree, not all of the fruit ripens at the same rate and on a single branch there can be under-ripe as well as ripe fruit. To produce consistently good-quality coffee, every cherry must be fully ripe, because those picked when under-ripe can contribute to harshness, lack of sweetness and even astringency in the roasted coffee. (Think of bananas at their still slightly green stage compared to perfectly ripe fruit.) Spotting a perfectly red cherry, without tinges of green, can be very difficult when trying to pick as much weight as possible. This is why pickers have to be carefully trained and incentivized on

quality-minded farms. It's also the reason that it can take up to 12 weeks to bring in the crop as it progressively ripens. Pickers may be sent out into the fields three times – sometimes more – to take cherries at their best. It's a huge area of cost for farms and one where, if prices are challenged, corners are cut and quality lost.

As each day's pickings arrive at the processing unit, they are tagged with the date and in some cases the farm or locality where they were picked and are processed as a separate batch. On some farms, such as the larger estates found in Brazil, Guatemala and other volume producers, these quantities may result in 20 or 30 sacks of finished coffee. In the case of smallholder communities such as in Rwanda, where the average household has around 300–500 trees, a daily picking might only result in one or two sacks' worth.

Below: Coffee cherries at various stages of ripening. Optimum ripeness is on the right. The point of perfect ripeness can be difficult to spot when the cherry is still on the tree.
Facing page (top left): Coffee picker at Emporium Farm, Panama; (top right) handfuls of ripe cherries; (bottom left) inspecting coffee trees at Abahuzamugambi Ba Kawa Cooperative, Huye, Rwanda; (bottom right) picking coffee, Chirripó region, Costa Rica.

PROCESSING

After the cherries are picked, and sorted to remove under-ripe fruit, the coffee beans (the seeds) need to be separated from the fruit, and then dried, so that they do not rot. Some coffee growers process their own fruit, while farmers who are members of a larger cooperative might deliver their cherries to a central washing or processing station. There are three commonly practised processing methods: the natural (dry), washed, and pulped natural (sometimes called honey) processes.

NATURAL (DRY) PROCESS

Traditionally practised where local conditions restrict access to water, or for historical reasons, this process takes the picked coffee cherries directly to the drying tables; the entire fruit is dried in the sun, for around 20 days. During this time, the bright red cherries shrivel as they lose moisture and turn black. (They need regular raking to ensure even drying and prevent mould and fermentation.)

When the cherries are dry and hard to the touch, the inner fruit has a raisin-like consistency. Machines separate the seeds from the fruit.

WASHED PROCESS

While still fresh from the field, the cherries may be hand-sorted on tables to remove any under-ripe fruit; often the cherries are then thrown into large water tanks where any immature cherries (where one bean inside failed to develop even though the fruit is red) float to the surface. These are skimmed off before the next stage: depulping. The depulping machine splits the cherry and separates the beans inside from the fruit pulp, which is collected in 'compost heaps' to rot down and be applied back to the soils as an organic improver. After depulping, the beans still carry a heavy coat of sticky pulp, or mucilage. They are left in another tank, covered by a plastic sheet, to ferment for around 12–24 hours while natural yeasts work on the sugars to break them down and release the remaining pulp from the seeds. Following a final washing in clean water, the beans are put out into the sun to dry. In Central and South America this is traditionally done on large patios, although producers are increasingly using raised tables, which lift the beans off the ground and improve air circulation. It's important to dry the coffee gently, not allowing it to become too hot, and this process can take up to 21 days.

Above: Ripe, red cherries drying for natural process coffee, Panama. Facing page (top): Honey process coffee drying at Los Lajones, Panama. The mucilage left on the beans (which may turn yellow or red depending on how much is retained) produces a sweeter, fuller-bodied cup; (bottom left) smallholder coffee farmer with his coffee at home, Bale, Ethiopia; (bottom right) the final stage in producing washed coffee, Maraba, Rwanda.

PULPED NATURAL OR HONEY PROCESS

First developed in Brazil to allow coffees to be used for a wider range of styles in the cup, this hybrid approach first depulps the coffee as in the washed process, but leaves the mucilage surrounding the beans while they dry in the sun. During the drying period, the sticky flesh turns darker and, depending upon the amount of mucilage left on, the beans are referred to as red honey (lots of mucilage left on) or yellow honey, where a thinner layer of mucilage is left behind.

THE EFFECT ON FLAVOUR

Each of these processing methods results in a different balance in the roasted coffee. After country of origin and roasting style, the processing method has the biggest impact upon the flavour of the coffee.

Fully washed coffees tend to demonstrate their acidity profile most clearly and have lighter- to medium-bodied expressions of their nature, with citrus fruit tones being most prominent.

Natural coffees have an altogether 'wilder' nature. They can be syrupy sweet, the fruit tones more comparable to cooked or stewed fruits, and even a mildly spicy or 'boozy' character when processed carefully.

Pulped natural or honey coffees combine the best of both methods. Acidities remain ample but may be perceived as being more gentle due to more sweetness being retained. For the same reason, these coffees exhibit syrupy sweet body and the widest span of flavour characteristics.

Moisture matters

Whichever processing method is used, the green beans must be dried to the point where their moisture content is at a maximum of 12.5 per cent. Anything higher than this and they are prone to mould growth and quality deterioration. Moisture should be measured with a moisture meter, but small-scale farmers may simply chew on a bean and, through their experience, tell how hard it is with their teeth and thereby determine the moisture content. Moisture levels will be measured again with meters when the beans arrive at the dry mill, and then again when they reach their final destination – the importer's warehouse or the roasters.

Resting

The processed beans, still inside their papery coat of dried skin (parchment), are stored for 30–60 days. This 'resting' period allows the flavour elements within the beans to mature and stabilize while moisture levels even out. The parchment layer acts as a temperature and moisture jacket, protecting each bean.

Finally, the beans are hulled (dry-milled) to remove the parchment, mechanically graded by size, and then bagged ready for shipping.

Top row (left to right): Washed parchment coffee drying on raised or African beds, Kabuye, Rwanda; coffee pulping at Maraba, Rwanda; coffee washing station at Maraba, Rwanda. In the background, the pulping area, fermentation tanks and pre-drying area; in the foreground, the warehouse and drying beds. Bottom row (left to right): Pre-sorting to remove under-ripe cherries before pulping, Maraba, Rwanda; parchment coffee initially dried on raised or African beds in the rear and then finished on patios in the foreground, MICEPA, Costa Rica; smallholder family pulping coffee cherries at their home, Rwanda.

CAFFEINE AND DECAFFEINATED COFFEE

Would you drink coffee if it didn't have caffeine in it? For some people the answer is a resounding 'not in a million years!' For others, caffeine is the part of coffee that they want (or need) to avoid. It's a central nervous system stimulant, and people have different tolerances for it. Some can't even drink the weakest tea without suffering severe after-effects. And some people love coffee but find that drinking it too late in the day gives them sleeping problems. (That's a physiological reality, as coffee persists in the system for some hours after it's drunk.)

What do you lose when you take caffeine out of coffee? It's more than just stimulation. Caffeine is an alkaloid, and it has a bitter flavour. Its role in the growing coffee bush is to act as a natural pesticide. The bitterness is part of the overall flavour profile of coffee, much in the same way that dark chocolate has an inherent bitterness. This is an adult, sophisticated taste – just think of how children prefer milk chocolate, but usually come to appreciate dark as they get older. We often use an analogy of bitterness being the shade that contrasts with the light (or the sweetness) in a picture. Can you have light without shade, good without evil, or sweetness without bitterness?

Funnily enough, if you have a low tolerance for caffeine, you are better off drinking espresso than a mug of filter- or drip-brewed coffee. The latter will have something like 120mg to 140mg of caffeine, while an espresso has around 70–90mg. This comes as a surprise to many people, who assume that the powerful, intense flavour of espresso translates into higher caffeine content. It isn't true – though obviously if you drank a mug of espresso you would be getting enough caffeine to set your heart racing and probably make your hair stand on end.

Is decaf the real deal?

Some people find that decaffeinated coffee is missing something fundamental to their enjoyment of the drink, and we are inclined to agree with them – though some decaf is perfectly good. Even with the most gentle decaf processing, it is inevitable that some character of the original coffee gets lost or muted. However, the main reason that decaf is so often disappointing is probably down to the cost of the additional processing along with transport costs to and from the decaffeination facility.

The process is performed by specialist companies because the equipment needed – and the size of the batches needed to be efficient – is outside the scope of most roasters. Large decaffeination companies usually purchase green coffee from the open market, process it and then sell the decaffeinated green coffee to brokers, who then sell on to roasters. In most cases, to keep costs down, the decaf companies do not buy the highest-quality green coffee to start with – so the result is effectively compromised from the beginning.

At Union we recognize that people who need to avoid caffeine deserve as good a cup of coffee as anyone. Our approach is therefore to select from our own purchases of high-quality green coffees and send these to our specialist decaffeinator in Germany who runs a bespoke batch for us before sending it back to our roastery.

A few years ago, we supplied a café that was opened by a health professional who wanted to promote healthy living. Among his ideas was that the coffee served would only be decaf – but he was determined *not* to mention this on the menu board. After six months, nobody had asked whether the coffee was decaf, and more than a few customers had complimented the owner on how good the coffee was!

The decaffeination process

Decaffeination of coffee was first carried out in 1903, by a German coffee merchant named Ludwig Roselius. He sold his coffee under the name Kaffee (later Café) HAG, and it became famous in France and the USA under the name Sanka (derived from the French *sans caféine*, 'without caffeine'). Roselius used benzene as a solvent. Chemical solvents are still used today, but benzene is generally not one of them because of associated health risks. There are three main methods today, each of which involves the use of a 'selective solvent'. All begin with green coffee beans, before they are roasted. And note that even decaf retains a tiny amount of caffeine, despite the name. (The legal definition of decaffeinated coffee is that it must be at least 98 per cent caffeine-free.)

SWISS WATER PROCESS

This process was first developed in the 1930s but was not widely used until much later. It begins by soaking the green beans in hot water to remove the caffeine – but in doing that, all the flavour also dissolves into the water. The water – now called a green coffee extract because it contains all those substances from the green beans – is passed through an activated charcoal filter to remove just the caffeine. Then another batch of green beans is soaked in the same water. Because the water is full of flavour-forming compounds, the flavour-forming compounds in the new batch remain in the beans; only caffeine is removed. This process is repeated until almost all the caffeine has been removed, then the beans are dried and are ready for roasting.

CHEMICAL SOLVENT PROCESSES

In these methods, the beans are steamed and then washed over many hours with a solvent, usually ethyl acetate, which removes the caffeine. The drained beans are then steamed again to remove the solvent, and dried in readiness for roasting. Ethyl acetate is a compound that occurs naturally in a number of foods, so coffee processed this way can be described as 'naturally decaffeinated'.

Hold the jitters: a 1920s British advertisement for the pioneering decaf Kaffee Hag.

CARBON DIOXIDE (CO_2) METHOD

Technically known as subcritical carbon dioxide extraction, this is the newest method for decaffeination. The beans are soaked in water and put in a sealed steel container, into which liquid CO_2 is then pumped under enormous pressure. The CO_2 dissolves the caffeine from the beans without affecting flavour-forming compounds. It is then drawn off to another container, where it reverts to a gas.

AROUND THE WORLD

More than 30 countries are today involved in the commercial cultivation and export of coffee, and many of them are increasingly able, in smaller or greater quantities, to produce the fine quality that we recognize as speciality coffee. This is defined as coffee that scores 80 points or above in a 100-point scale (see page 97) created by the Specialty Coffee Association of America (SCAA) and recognized by all involved in the coffee trade worldwide; lower grades of coffee are described as commodity coffee. In this section we will explore some of our favourites that have become regulars at our London roastery. Using these introductions as a starting point, your own tastings will determine your personal preferences. We find that once you're attuned to the sweetness and vibrancy of freshly roasted high-quality coffee, buying a new coffee that you have never tasted becomes an adventure and delight. This is much more enjoyable than thinking you have to find 'the one' right coffee for you.

Country and region

Does it matter where your coffee beans come from? It most certainly does. Harvesting a kilo of cherries and processing them into exportable coffee beans is done differently in Guatemala, Ethiopia or Panama. Each country has its own practices and customs. Each also has its own traditional varieties and microclimates, resulting in unique flavour profiles that differ from country to country.

Those differences also affect the price you end up paying as a consumer. In each country farmers are subject to certain conditions: not just socio-economic situations but also country-related risks. A sustainable price for a coffee from Guatemala will be different to one from Costa Rica. The quoted or published world market price for coffee does not take into account quality and country-specific situations, so once traded, shipped and roasted, coffees from some countries may turn out to be more expensive than those from other countries.

Within each country, stating the region where coffee is grown is important and relates to the varieties grown, geography and microclimate of the area. At the quality end of the coffee market, with careful growing, harvesting and processing, these regional and local factors have a significant influence upon the cup character and can be a useful reference for buyers and consumers.

Facing page, top row (left to right): Juliana Mendoza Pablo, cooperative member of Esquipulas Cooperative, Huehuetenango, Guatemala; Jeremy Torz getting in the way at Esquipulas Producers, Guatemala. Note the local dress of jacket and striped trousers; parchment coffee resting in a warehouse, Rwanda. Centre: Rwanda, 'The Land of 1000 Hills'. Bottom row (left to right): Roadside coffee stall, Ethiopia; village children in rural Rwanda.

AFRICA AND ARABIA

Coffee is produced in 20 African countries, but the combination of high quality and significant exports is still a relative rarity. In the following pages we have highlighted the countries that are currently most prominent on the export stage. These are most notably to be found around the Great Rift Valley – particularly in Ethiopia and Kenya, as well as in Burundi, Rwanda and Tanzania – where the topography is significantly more mountainous and offers large expanses of cooler highlands where Arabica may thrive.

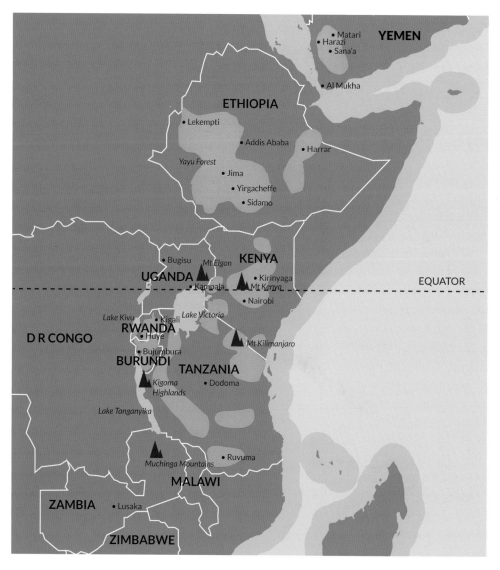

Main coffee-growing regions

Other countries in Africa and Arabia do make an impact in other ways. There are thousands of small-scale farmers in **Democratic Republic of the Congo**, most growing Robusta, but in the east, closer to the border with Rwanda and around Lake Kivu, efforts are being made to cultivate land for Arabica. At higher altitudes the DRC certainly has the potential to yield good quality, although low market prices and regional conflict have worked against development of a sustainable industry with good market connections. **Uganda** is the second largest coffee producer in Africa (after Ethiopia) but this is entirely due to Robusta, of which it is the world's second largest producer after Vietnam. Only around 10 per cent of the country's coffee is Arabica and most of this comes from a region around Mount Elgon in the east, close to the Kenyan border, from where it is relatively easy to export. **Malawi** is another country with great potential, but the best coffees are produced in very small quantities and are hard to find on the international market. **Zambia** also has great potential, growing Arabica (often Bourbon) mostly on large farms in the north-eastern districts at the southern end of Lake Tanganyika. Cup quality is still recovering from the effects of mass planting of a disease-resistant strain called Catimor in the 1970s – it is not as sweet or flavourful as Bourbon or other local hybrids and has not found a place in the speciality market. Production in **Zimbabwe** fell dramatically with the agricultural reforms instituted early in the present century and is still well down on historic levels. Established as a commercial producer in the 1960s, Zimbabwe exported small quantities of truly fine Arabica coffees that showed some of the quality aspects of Kenya AA (see page 35). But here, as elsewhere in Africa, the prospect of economic and political stability would do much to stimulate production.

Flavour profiles from African coffees are incredibly diverse – probably offering the broadest spectrum of any continent. Ethiopia alone is capable of producing coffees ranging from spicy and winy Harrars to lemon-floral and bergamot Yirgacheffes. Kenya is renowned for blackcurrant and boldly sharp acidities, which contrast with the more voluptuous orange-chocolate notes of Rwanda. The continent's best coffees make it a great place to explore and they are often easy to differentiate for beginners and seasoned drinkers alike.

Burundi

Belgian colonists established coffee here around 1930. For many years, up until the conflict of 1994, which resulted in the regional displacement of hundreds of thousands of people, coffee formed the principal export. The industry then moved into a period of public ownership when the government, through World Bank-financed projects, invested in many coffee washing stations (post-harvest processing centres). This meant that key parts of the process could be better managed for quality. More recently the industry has been partly privatized and new rules created to liberalize export licences. The benefit is that instead of all coffees being bulked up into one 'national' style, we can now select from distinct regions and find coffees that range from rich, full-bodied, nutty and caramel styles to those from higher altitudes and with better processing that yield a very drinkable tangerine-citrus and chocolate balance.

Much of the coffee is Bourbon. As in Rwanda this helps to differentiate it from other East African countries. Smallholder production is the norm with most households working 300–800 trees on plots of around a quarter of a hectare and producing around 30kg of exportable coffee per year. Since around 2009, a newly energized world market has seen great interest in new origins among consumers. Burundi, like its neighbour Rwanda, has capitalized effectively upon this with annual quality competitions now attracting speciality coffee buyers from around the world.

We are fortunate to have a relationship, since 2004, with Yirgacheffe Coffee Farmers Cooperative Union, particularly Konga Cooperative. Their coffee is grown in small family plots and referred to as 'garden coffee'. More recently we've pioneered coffees from the Yayu Forest region, where Union Direct Trade has worked alongside development agencies to enhance farmers' incomes and to help with managing deforestation – a significant challenge for Ethiopia and other coffee-growing countries.

Ethiopia

Ethiopia has more coffee-growing regions and distinct flavour profiles than almost any other country. From its position as the birthplace of Arabica coffee, cultivation has been under way here for centuries and thanks largely to the traditional practice of growing locally (and not trading seeds between different parts of the country) it has preserved strong regional differences – from the winy and spicy style of Harrar in the east, to the jasmine-floral and bergamot notes of Yirgacheffe in the south, and on to Sidamo, Jima (Djimmah), Lekempti, each with subtle or bolder variations of spicy, floral, winy, nutty and chocolate notes.

Ethiopia is a difficult country to fulfil through Union Direct Trade. Around 80 per cent of Ethiopian coffee exports are administered through the Ethiopian Commodity Exchange (ECX), an auction system that gives access to exporters and offers farmers a market outlet for their coffee. Only cooperatives and large privately owned farms that are able to process their own coffee can sell outside ECX. However, the time gap between harvest and export (and payment) can be several weeks. Many farmers therefore opt to sell their coffee to ECX because they get paid the next day. In the ECX system, coffees are mixed on the basis of grades (size) and it becomes difficult to know where the coffee came from. The outcome is that a lot of good coffees become anonymous or get lost in a blend.

Kenya

Kenya, with its leading designation Kenya AA, is among the world's most famous coffees. A coffee industry was established here from the early 20th century; after independence in 1963 the Kenyans, having understood the potential value of their coffee, continued to capitalize on the knowledge developed under colonial rule. Though mostly growing modern cultivars rather than the original Bourbon thought to have been taken there from Réunion in the late 19th century, Kenya has pioneered some varieties with exceptional quality (as well as some recent rust-resistant hybrids). These are increasingly being seen in other parts of the world as a new generation of farmers experiments with drought resistance as well as cup quality.

The best regions are not far from the capital, Nairobi, on the slopes of Mount Kenya in the

Nyeri and Kirinyaga districts. As Kenya has held its reputation, country premiums for its coffees are high and much of the bulk industry has looked elsewhere. To remain competitive, however, many larger operations have cut costs – with inevitable reduction in cup quality. Although it is possible to buy directly from very well managed large farms and traditional estates, these rarely offer the quality we require at the speciality end of the coffee trade. More commonly, the mills that prepare the coffees for export operate as the end business, buying from small farms and cooperative enterprises. With this type of operator, we can find the path back to each contributing farmer and ensure that the cash reward goes to them and does not get lost somewhere within the government export board.

At their best, Kenya coffees exhibit a bright, juicy acidity, with fruit tones redolent of blackcurrant and a heady, fruity, sweet aroma. There are some jewels out there, but owing to the lack of transparency in the market (and some corruption), they are increasingly hard to find or trade ethically.

A WORD ABOUT AA

The supposed top designation of quality in Kenya is the AA mark. All coffees prepared for export must be tasted by a government-approved taster, or liquorer. Coffee beans merely have to be of a certain physical size to qualify for AA status, so it is not a true mark of quality, and in reality, many quality levels exist within AA. Cup quality may be reduced in the smaller beans, but AB, the second grade, can offer some value-for-money surprises.

Rwanda

Rwanda was faced with having to virtually restart its coffee industry after the genocidal conflict in 1994. Coffee had been responsible for 70 per cent of the country's export trade, but the sector was plagued with poor organization and the coffees of Rwanda were unknown outside of the commodity coffee trade. Rwanda's coffee sold on the international market under the name Rwanda Ordinaire and frequently only to institutional companies for instant coffee or low-cost blends.

Around 2001, a friend who had been to Rwanda as part of a charity programme commented to us that he'd seen a lot of coffee growing but had never heard about it. Had we? After a couple of speculative visits we were hooked. 'The Land of 1000 Hills', as Rwanda is known, was perfectly placed to produce high-quality coffee. Most was original Bourbon variety, virtually unique in Africa and – if quality systems could be developed – offering an identity quite distinct from other African countries.

Over the following years, we worked alongside an NGO funded by USAID (United States Agency for International Development) to buy the coffee produced by the country's first new washing station (for post-harvest processing), and to participate in professional cupper training and farmer outreach. In 2009 the country organized its first quality competition and in 2010 it became the first African nation to host the prestigious Cup Of Excellence competition, a great achievement.

Today there are numerous washing stations in both cooperative and private hands and larger companies are entering the market with quality as well as quantity clearly in mind.

The coffees of Rwanda are produced throughout much of the country. Most notable areas to date are Huye in the south, the highlands around the shores of Lake Kivu in the west, and around the Ngoma Lakes region in the east. With increasing quality being realized every season, the coffees are characterized by cane-sugar sweetness, gentle orange-tangerine or even grape-like acidity and a milk-chocolate and caramel finish.

THEOPHILE BIZIYAREMYE

GENERAL MANAGER, COOPERATIVE ABAHUZAMUGAMBI BA KAWA (MARABA), HUYE, RWANDA

The Abahuzamugambi Ba Kawa Cooperative manages the activities of four coffee-washing stations in the Huye district of southern Rwanda. The district used to be called Maraba and officially the area is called Huye, but the name Maraba has stuck, both locally and internationally. In 2000, this group of farmers was selected to participate in a USAID-supported programme to improve the livelihoods of rural communities by producing high-quality coffee. The cooperative now has over 1500 members, many of whom cultivate fewer than 500 coffee trees. It provides a range of benefits to members, such as medical insurance, and advances money for school fees (obligatory in Rwanda), which producers can pay back in coffee cherries. It can provide credit in cases of emergency or a special event such as a wedding, and these credits too can be repaid with coffee cherries. There is a centre where villagers can use the internet and take computer courses. Theophile Biziyaremye has an economics degree from the National University of Rwanda in Butare, and has been General Manager for seven years.

'My family started farming coffee in 1975. I was born in 1980 and my first memory of coffee is of receiving money for selling unprocessed coffee cherries. I have been a coffee farmer since 2003 and became a cooperative member in 2004. We are in one of the poorest districts of a poor country, and coffee is generally the only way our farmers can

Steven with Theophile Biziyaremye, general manager of Abahuzamugambi Cooperative, and Angelique Karekezi, managing director of RWASHOSCCO, Maraba, Rwanda.

earn any cash. When the cooperative started many of us lived in single-room homes built from mud bricks, with a tin roof and a dirt floor. Coffee now allows me to feed my family and build a good home. It paid for my education, and it will pay for my children's education.

When the project started, researchers realized that our coffee trees were of the Bourbon variety, a heritage type with excellent flavour profile. However, each household did its own post-harvest processing, which introduced many variables and defects. The project built a processing facility, where farmers deliver coffee cherries that are prepared to a high and consistent standard. This transformed the quality. From other regions and countries I have learned more about using fertilizers and pesticides to increase production and produce better coffee. We use pyrethrum-based insecticides, which are derived from plants (and are permitted in organic farming). Good coffee starts in good farming and continues in good processing. By increasing quality alongside productivity, we can achieve a good price. And working together with farmers and buyers enables us to bring our coffee to market easily and, I hope, satisfy the demands of the customers.'

Tanzania

A long tradition of coffee growing exists in some regions of Tanzania, but local practices and preferences clashed with the 20th-century commercial views of European colonists. Together with a lack of organization and investment, this meant that the industry had failed to develop in terms of quality until very recently. Today, most coffee is grown by smallholders with 3–5 hectares (7–12 acres) per family.

There are areas with high mountain terrain, good soils and bountiful rainfall, which are capable of producing outstanding quality coffees. The best areas seem to be around Kilimanjaro in the north-east, adjacent to the Kenyan border; Ruvuma on the southern Mozambique border; and the Kigoma highlands to the west.

One of the main challenges in bringing new high-quality coffees to the market is that consumers tend to purchase what they know, and as Tanzania has not really gained much in the way of international exposure, market uptake is still relatively low. This is a situation that needs to change.

With careful processing, Tanzania's coffee can be wonderfully sweet, juicy, complex, full-bodied and a great representation of African coffee – if you can find it!

Yemen

After Ethiopia, Yemen is by far the oldest centre of civilization in the world in which coffee has been continuously cultivated. Due to the plant's early arrival from Ethiopia, harsh local conditions and a tradition that left varieties established in their districts, many sub-varieties developed as a consequence of local adaptation. These different strains and the somewhat haphazard method by which the cherries are picked and processed are responsible for a unique style and character. At their best, the coffees are full-bodied and syrupy with winy, spicy (thyme, clove, and even hints of cumin) and sometimes gamey flavours that make for a highly aromatic and rich cup with a distinctive chocolate finish. Some say that as the coffee was originally shipped out through the port of Mocha (Al Mukha) the word became synonymous with the chocolate character.

The principal growing areas are found in a strip to the west of the capital Sana'a and are extremely arid highland regions where the coffee trees are terraced into the steep mountain slopes and irrigated by traditional hand-dug trenches fed by deep wells. The names to look out for are Matari, Sana'a and Harazi: the varieties are named after the localities in which they developed. It is not unusual, however, for many of these to be mixed at export, probably enhancing the overall complexity of the coffee.

Due to their great rarity (only around 150,000 bags are produced annually), the coffees of Yemen sell for a very high price. Authentication is a real concern and it's not uncommon for coffees to be passed through many hands, with a little customization at each stage. Over the years, we have managed to develop trusted partners in the country and often airfreight small parcels direct to avoid any problems.

Since 2013 the political situation has sadly made direct trade with Yemen almost impossible for us.

ASIA AND OCEANIA

We often think of Indonesia as producing the 'big red wines' of the coffee world. Their style of low acidity promotes long-finishing, heavy-bodied and slightly peaty or smoky cups perfect for the colder seasons of the year when you want a roaring fire and something to cuddle up with! Java and Sumatra are Indonesia's main coffee producers, and Arabica coffee is also grown on other islands, including Sulawesi and Bali. These far-flung islands include some of the most distinctive coffees in the world, often due to particular local adaptations of processing techniques. Certain strains of Timor hybrid, an Arabica-Robusta cross, bred to produce high-yielding trees, result in a heavy, slightly woody cup style with low acidity that gives a sense of smoothness not seen in Latin American or East African coffees.

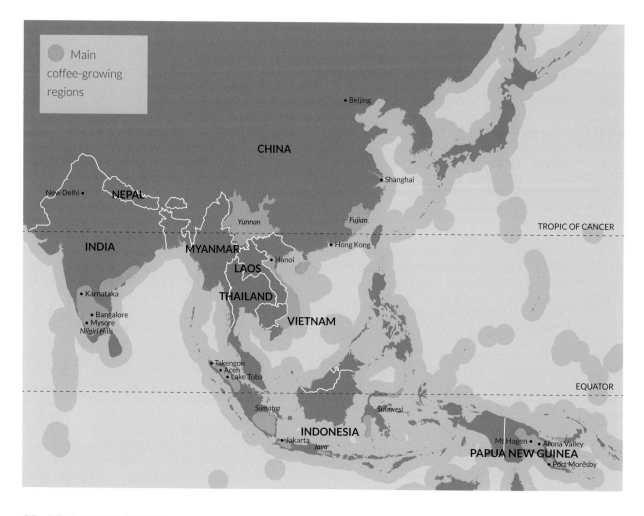

Main coffee-growing regions

CHINA
• Beijing
New Delhi • NEPAL
• Shanghai
Yunnan
Fujian
TROPIC OF CANCER
INDIA   MYANMAR   • Hong Kong
• Hanoi
LAOS
• Karnataka
THAILAND
• Bangalore
• Mysore   VIETNAM
Nilgiri Hills
• Takengon
• Aceh
• Lake Toba
EQUATOR
Sumatra   Sulawesi
INDONESIA   Mt Hagen •   • Arona Valley
• Jakarta   PAPUA NEW GUINEA
Java   • Port Moresby

This interesting picture is not maintained throughout the region, however: while Papua New Guinea has great potential, China is still evolving, and in India and Vietnam the emphasis is on commodity-level Robusta coffee.

Robusta may not be to the taste of fine coffee drinkers but in **Myanmar (Burma)**, **Laos** and **Thailand** it can be a saviour. Coffee has been encouraged as a replacement crop for opium in the Golden Triangle, and Thailand's production is quite substantial – larger than that of Kenya. In the northern areas close to the Laos and Burma borders, efforts are being made to improve quality and concentrate on Arabica. Another country that currently has a tiny production but may be worth watching is **Nepal**, which has the right altitude for growing high-quality Arabica, although limitations of transport infrastructure makes it very difficult to export, and passage through such dramatic altitude and temperatures ranges during transport also have a deleterious effect upon the coffees long before they get to the roaster.

Australia grows only Arabica – absolutely tiny quantities of it – in Queensland state in the country's north-east. Although the farms lie (just) within the equatorial bands suited to coffee growing, lack of altitude means that acidity profiles do not really develop in the cup; though clean and mild, the coffees often lack any particular distinction. Local wages also have an impact on saleability: in a country paying 'western' living wages, the cost is high and this tends to consign Australia-grown coffee to curiosity purchases.

Smallholder farmer in Sulawesi drying coffee at home before sending to the mill for final processing and grading.

China

Coffee has become a significant part of daily life here as global trends are adopted in this increasingly prosperous and populous country. Quietly and without much international scrutiny, China is now estimated to be the world's 14th largest producer, broadly on the scale of Costa Rica, with around 1.8 million bags per year. Very little is exported, but far from having a big national habit, when imports and net exports are averaged across 1.4 billion people, per capita annual consumption is estimated at 5 or 6 cups per year, the majority being soluble coffee. The trend for fresh coffee is expected to grow and western-style coffee shops are increasingly common in major cities, with not only familiar international franchises but some very good home-grown operations.

Coffee was introduced in Yunnan province by a French missionary in the late 19th century, but it was virtually ignored until 1998, when the United Nations, World Bank and the Chinese government saw the opportunity to develop the industry. With the support of multinational coffee companies, volumes exploded. The coffee is predominantly Arabica in Yunnan, with smaller amounts of Robusta in the coastal Fujian province. Varieties are predominantly Catimor, a lower-quality Robusta-based hybrid, although a move to seek higher value coffees has seen more plantings of Bourbon and Typica. The quality of the coffee does not yet achieve speciality grade. Most is sold to the large multinationals; Germany, home to many international roast, ground and soluble brands, is the largest importer.

India

India was an early waypoint for coffee in its journey out of Africa and on to the rest of the world. Legend has it that a pilgrim named Baba Budan smuggled just seven seeds out of Yemen and in 1675 returned to the district of Chikmagalur in southern Karnataka state on the eastern fringes of the Western Ghats mountain range. Today the district most known for coffee is south of Mysore in the Nilgiri hills, where it competes for land with India's main cultivated crop, tea.

The modern coffee industry in India is focused on Robusta rather than Arabica as the climate and altitude profile is much more suited to the prolific but lower-grade cousin. A lack of added value has been a challenge to quality improvement and investment as most of the Arabica coffee is smallholder-produced, with very poor traceability back to the farmers. Without this key aspect, producers cannot trade on the intrinsic value of their crops and have to accept the 'going rate' regardless of the quality of their coffee.

Even with market liberalizations, the structure of the industry and particularly its export processing mean that it is still very difficult to be confident of exactly who grew the coffee and, in the case of an outstanding lot, to be able to find where it came from and actively seek it out again.

The flavour profile of Indian coffees comes mainly from locally developed hybrids that were created to be more disease-resistant. The primary characteristics are for medium- to full-bodied coffees with slightly woody or almond-butter nutty tones and very low acidity that emphasizes the soft, sometimes creamy, nature of the cup.

A 'curiosity' of Indian coffee that remains popular among coffee drinkers of a certain age in the UK is Monsooned Malabar. This shares characteristics with the Indonesian aged coffees known as Old Brown Java and it arose in much the same way. Its production is now carried out in a more modern, controlled manner and is centred on the rainy season, when large open-sided barns are racked out with the coffee beans to expose them to moisture.

Indonesia

JAVA

The biggest name historically in Indonesian coffee was Java. As a staple of the Dutch East India Company, Java coffee's ubiquity in the market led it to become a common name for the brew. Although Java once held the reputation for quality among Indonesian coffees, its star has long fallen. The industry there is today mostly centred upon very large government-run estates which chase the volume market. The small number of independent producers are not organized in a way that makes their coffee traceable when traded. In recent years, Java has almost completely disappeared from the speciality coffee market as more refined Sumatra coffees have attracted the buyers..

In the UK one of the 'curiosities' of the Indonesian coffee trade was 'Old Brown Java', a name that is still sometimes seen in more 'traditional' coffee retailers. The style came about through the tradition of using coffee as ballast in the sailing ships that brought it to the UK. In the damp conditions of the holds, the coffee absorbed moisture and, when dried, yielded a very mellow brew – if also somewhat woody and musty smelling! The coffee that had been through the 'process' lost all of its acidity, and, coupled with the woodiness and dark roasting, seemed to appeal to the coffee drinkers of the late 17th and early 18th centuries. The practice of 'maturing' the coffee through exposure to moist conditions continued. This process is also used in India, where the coffee is called Monsooned Malabar, but it is accomplished on land and under much more controlled conditions.

SUMATRA

Sumatra seems to go through phases of coming in to and out of fashion, which is probably more to do with what's happening in other coffee countries than for any reason connected with its coffee. Sumatra has a unique approach to processing its coffee after harvest, removing all layers of skin and parchment while still wet, a process called *giling basah*. The beans have a moisture content of over 35 per cent at this stage. They are taken from householder farmers by a local collector, who amasses enough to take to the mill. It's at this stage, while still moist, that the coffees acquire most of their unique character. Processing accounts for a great deal of the style: sometimes smoky, woody or even with a hint of earthiness and spice and tobacco notes. The unroasted beans are off-green with a bluish hue, different from most other green coffees from Africa or Latin America. The beans often appear irregular or with bits chipped off them.

In recent years, we have worked hard to try to understand the inherent character of the coffee as opposed to the characteristics conferred by the process. It is possible now to work directly with small groups and to export their beans without government interference. With additional care in processing it is possible to produce coffees from Sumatra that retain just enough 'origin character' in the processing style but to balance that with the finer elements that the plants and soil are responsible for. Perhaps think of peaty whisky from Islay – some are beasts and all you get is the peat smoke, others are more subtly nuanced. The second kind – that's the cup we want from Sumatra.

Most of the quality coffee is grown and produced around Lake Toba and further north, up into the tip of Aceh province around Takengon. Don't look for Mandehling – it's a marketing term for a collection centre and these coffees don't now represent anything like the best of Sumatra.

Papua New Guinea

Coffee was first planted by colonial growers on estate farms in the 1920s. In recent decades production has decentralized and smallholders are now responsible for over 90 per cent of exports. They tend to work as cooperatives or producer associations, but making quality improvements is very difficult because of the challenging terrain, difficult access on the highland roads and lack of equipment. As a result, the coffee can range from very good to very average: consistency is often the missing factor. Happily, recent enhancement of relationships between producers and roasters in Australia, the nearest market, are having a positive impact and we can hope for better to come.

Coffees from Papua New Guinea go in and out of fashion in different markets. In the USA, where these coffees have an established following, the majority comes from the larger private estates, most notably Sigri, in the Western Highlands around Mount Hagen, as well as the Arona Valley in the Eastern Highlands. Most of the production reaching European markets increasingly comes from the smallholder producers, with all of their challenges, and this may be why PNG coffees have failed so far to maintain their following and reputation. But they deserve wider recognition, as they have a pleasant character midway between those heavier coffees of Indonesia and the lighter styles of South American Bourbon mild coffees. At their best, the coffees can be medium-creamy-bodied with a gentle balance of peach-like sweet acidity and a soft nutty-caramel finish.

Vietnam

Coffee was first grown in Vietnam in the 19th century under French colonial rule, but the country's importance as a producer began in the mid-1980s, when the government recognized coffee's potential as a cash-earning export crop. Since then, Vietnam has become the second largest producer in the world, its output exceeded only by that of Brazil. This has been good news for the Vietnamese economy in the near term, though the destruction of forest land to plant coffee bushes may be storing a longer-term problem for the country. (The same thing is happening in neighbouring Laos.)

Vietnam does not produce quality Arabica and has largely served to destabilize world markets with oversupply of both Robusta and Arabica. As many of the multinationals buy coffee on price and with only a passing nod to character, the vast production developed after the mid-1990s allowed the world's big players to shop around for ever-cheaper supplies regardless of origin. Or quality.

Mountainous terrain in the region of Mount Hagen, Papua New Guinea. Many of the hill tribes in this region still lead very traditional lives in both dress and housing.

CENTRAL AMERICA AND THE CARIBBEAN

Much of this region is paradise for coffee trees, and some of its producing nations are among the best in the world. Perfect balances of rainfall and sun, and altitude ranges offering huge expanses of mountain forest above 1500m (5000ft), enable these coffees to be some of the most alluring to be found. When combined with good production techniques, the beans give clean, well-developed fruit and acidities that offer complexities similar to the most elegant white wines. The best Central American coffees have bright zesty fruit acidities ranging from sweet lemon to peach and apricot stone fruit. Usually forward on the palate, they delight with a sense of freshness and candy sweetness.

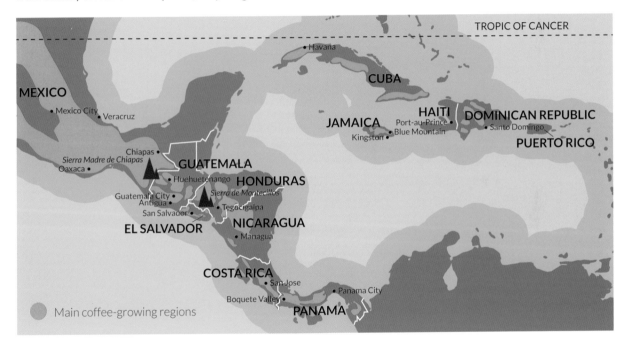

Main coffee-growing regions

Two countries that were once important producers have seen their output plummet. A major exporter in the 19th century, **Puerto Rico** has dropped out of sight in large part because there are not enough pickers – the country 'suffers' from high local costs as it comes under the employment law of the USA. In the years before Hurricane Mitch in 1998, one or two boutique producers, most notably Yauco Selecto, established highly controlled harvesting and processing facilities that produced some very clean and aromatic coffees that sold well in the US speciality market. Following the hurricane, and coupled with a market crash in the early 2000s, production struggled to return and markets had already been lost to other producing nations. **Haiti** was once an even more important producer, but the industry has steadily shrunk. In both countries, the potential is there waiting to be rediscovered.

Costa Rica

In 1816 this small Central American country became the first to establish a flourishing coffee industry. The first coffee export to England, in 1832, was via Chile under the name Café Valparaiso. From 1846 to 1890 coffee was Costa Rica's only export product and it continues to be a very important crop.

As a relatively small producer (exporting around 1.8 million 60kg bags versus Brazil's 45 million) the country has adopted a march for quality and differentiation among speciality producers who cannot compete with the low-cost bigger nations. In recent years many producers who previously sold to their local mill have constructed their own micro-mills. In addition to allowing full traceability this has enabled farmers to innovate and focus on quality.

The country is divided into eight diverse and extremely fertile coffee regions: Guanacaste, West Valley, Central Valley, Tres Ríos,

Turrialba, Orosi, Tarrazú, Brunca. Costa Rica is unique in containing virtually all of the climate and terrain profiles, from coastal (both Atlantic and Pacific) up to cloud forest and high mountain peaks and is therefore recognized as having the greatest biodiversity of just about any country on the planet.

Costa Rica's coffees are some of the world's brightest and sweetest, and are at best famed for their clarity and transparent flavours. They're usually light- to medium-bodied in style, but newer honey processing methods now being used are adding to the diversity and weight of their flavours.

Coffee trees growing under shade, Finca Santa Emiliana, Tres Ríos, Costa Rica. Taller trees are planted to give dappled shade which protects the coffee trees from the full heat of the sun.

Cuba

Today, Cuba is probably better known for rum and sugar than for coffee, but that was not always so. First introduced in the late 18th century, the coffee tree found a home in the eastern and southern regions, where higher altitudes and more temperate conditions allowed it to flourish. By 1820 Cuba's coffee was mainly exported to Spain, France and Germany, where it was traded at a quality premium and contributed even more to Cuba's national income than sugar. Its importance continued up until the revolution in 1959, when farms were nationalized and the industry went into decline. In an effort to rejuvenate, large coffee zones were established using volunteer labour instead of established and knowledgeable farmers. Lack of investment, infrastructure and a professional commercial approach, together with the climatic conditions (high rainfall during the periods when coffee needs to be sun-dried), continue to challenge quality coffee production. Cubans drink more coffee than they grow, and with the world's biggest market off-limits due to the US trade embargo, little opportunity is seen within the country.

Many tasting notes written on Cuban coffee cite chocolate and nutty tones in the brew along with hints of tobacco. Having never really found this latter nuance ourselves, we wonder if it's more about the cigar romance of Cuba than the actual taste!

Despite the weather challenges, there is no doubt that the Caribbean climate and great soils present here could, with the right support, produce some interesting coffees. Altitudes are somewhat lower than many Central American regions and acidity profiles in the coffees are gentle, much like those of Brazil. At Union we are yet to make it to Cuba, but admit to it being very high up on our to-do list, especially as Jeremy has a more than passing interest in both rum and cigars.

Dominican Republic

Very little of this country's coffee is exported: most is drunk by the islanders themselves. Even though it has never achieved the status of Jamaica, the coffee, if very carefully processed after harvesting, does have potential to offer a gentle, balanced cup with mild nutty, chocolate and berry fruit tones and delicate acidity profiles.

The main coffee growing regions of Cibao in the north and Bani, Ocoa and Barahona in the south, are situated on either side of a central mountain range that runs east to west and provides a range of altitudes and a virtually continuous rainy season. The temperate conditions and lack of a defined wet season promote coffee flowering almost year-round and a long main harvest period between November and June each year. The wide rainfall pattern causes challenges for the steady drying of fine coffees, and this, coupled with a lack of market-facing quality management, means that Dominican coffees have over the years often failed to achieve their potential. This may be the reason that the coffees have missed out on the Caribbean spotlight and price premium that Jamaica's coffees achieve.

View of the volcanic mountain range, Sierra Madre de Chiapas, Huehuetenango, Guatemala.

El Salvador

Coffee production in El Salvador has fuelled the Salvadoran economy and shaped its history for more than a century, but its success in today's speciality market has been driven by what must be one of the only beneficial effects of the country's long civil war that raged between 1979 and 1992.

Before the outbreak of conflict in 1978, El Salvador produced 3,381,000 bags of coffee on a largely feudal land ownership system with few rights for the indigenous population. During the years of conflict, production fell to below 1,000,000 bags and it was during this time that other regional producing countries modernized their industries, adopting newer high-yield cultivars that optimized their export volumes. These higher yields, however, often came with a drop-off in cup quality. After the civil war ended, it was recognized that El Salvador still retained the 'legendary' Bourbon heritage varietal along with another unique local variety called Pacas.

Today, these local varieties are producing full-bodied, roundly sweet coffees with wonderful red-fruit tones. We have been very fortunate to work with several excellent farmers who produce small lots of exceptional quality. These farmers have been part of a USAID project aimed at improving the quality of the lives of coffee producers by raising the quality of their coffee.

Guatemala

Guatemala is a spectacular country, particularly through the southern and western mountain ranges of the Sierra Madre de Chiapas and the western highlands of Huehuetenango. Blessed with many and varied microclimates, ideal rainfall patterns, majestic and high mountain ranges, and a great diversity of rich soils, these terrains have resulted in eight well-defined coffee producing regions. And while Colombia was marketing its one national output, Guatemala was romancing the trade with these distinct regions and a well-developed representation of a real portfolio of styles, ranging from lighter orange/citrus-bright and light- to medium-bodied, to the fuller-bodied and more red-wine and chocolate tones of San Marcos. The main varieties grown are Bourbon, Typica, Catuai and Caturra.

The eight regions are: Acatenango, Antigua, Atitlán, Cobán, Fraijanes, Huehuetenango, Nuevo Oriente and San Marcos. The most famous of these is Antigua. But with the recent rise of the other regions, most notably Huehuetenango (way-way-ten-AHN-go), where high altitude and an almost perfect balance of rainy and dry seasons develops coffee with rich fruity layers and great clarity, some question the premiums that Antigua's coffees still realize. We now source much of our Guatemalan coffee from Huehuetenango but also dip into others for our micro-lot selections: some regions are now recognized by official Protected Denomination of Origin (PDO) status.

Recognizing the importance of higher altitude in producing the finest coffees, Guatemala grades by altitude, with the highest grown being designated as SHB (Strictly Hard Bean), the next down the slope being SHG (Strictly High Grown).

ILIANA MARTÍNEZ

GENERAL MANAGER, COOPERATIVA ESQUIPULAS, LA LIBERTAD, HUEHUETENANGO, GUATEMALA

Esquipulas is a cooperative in the highlands of Huehuetenango, When we met them in 2009 they were in an unsuccessful trade relationship. They had put effort into training farmers, improving the cooperative and the quality of their coffee, but were unable to reach markets willing to pay a price premium for their coffee. Since then their export volumes have increased 2.5 times over, and they have established sustainable prices for their coffee. This cooperative works outside the Fairtrade system and has been able invest significantly in its community. A doctor provides free medical care for the community every Saturday and a pharmacy provides medicine at low cost. Iliana Martínez has played an instrumental role in the cooperative's development.

'My father was a farmer and also worked as a driver for the local priest, who gave him a small plot of land with coffee trees. Even as a young girl I occasionally worked on the farm, which grew coffee and also corn for our family to eat. It was fun seeking identical coffee beans in the cherries – we called them twins (cuaches) and we kept them as good luck charms.

When I was older I began to understand the economic significance of coffee in all its manifestations. The traditional coffee trade shows widespread injustice and inequality worldwide, as big companies live off the labour of producers. I already understood the effort and risk families faced in producing coffee, and when I studied in the USA I saw the price of a cup of coffee in a café. I realized then how disrespectful this was to coffee producers, who are not able to set the prices for their coffee. The system expected farmers to participate in the sector without any guarantee of being able to live with dignity.

Farmers require training in how to plan and manage their resources and maintain the quality of their coffee. Consumers need to see that coffee production is part of the culture and life of a community. It is the most important, often the only, income for the farmers and their families. The industry is still dominated by large coffee chains that may not focus on quality. Fortunately, special initiatives and ethical markets are growing and demanding the development of an alternative, fairer trading system that seeks to benefit all. But there is still much to achieve.'

Iliana Martínez (centre), the general manager of Esquipulas Cooperative, with members of the cooperative.

Honduras mainly produces commodity coffee but has increased earnings by developing many certified mills under Fairtrade and other schemes. Higher-quality coffee is also beginning to appear on the market, more of interest to premium-quality roasters.

Honduras

In the early 19th century, coffee established itself as an important export crop for Honduras, along with bananas. As a result of the country's challenging climate, the coffees did not fare well in retaining their character and became destined mostly for the commodity market. The industry appeared to be in hibernation, with very little infrastructure, until after 1975, when the major Brazil frost drove market prices higher and the government saw its opportunity to develop the country's value-added coffees. Between the late 1970s and 2000, crops increased from around half a million bags to just under 2 million, and by 2014 Honduras was around number 10 in the world league table at just under 3 million bags exported.

New drying techniques using poly-tunnel-type structures allow the hand-picked smallholder coffees to be dried more gently after fermentation and washing, with less risk of damage by rain. With the support of regional cupping labs set up by the government coffee organization, much more information and control is now available to farmers and quality is really improving. A good proportion of Bourbon and Typica varietals and a number of high-altitude growing areas above 1200m (4000ft) in the Sierra de Montecillos (in the south-west of the country) produce coffees with rich fruity depth and complex juicy acidity.

Hawaii

Coffees grown on the volcanic slopes of Mauna Loa in the south-west of the Big Island are known as Kona and are one of the most famous and expensive in the world (along with Jamaica Blue Mountain). Though established in the 19th century, it was not until the late 20th century that coffee began to be fully commercialized. Workers are subject to US labour law, so it is far from being a low-cost producer. Coupled with its relative scarcity in the market (exports are around 45,000–50,000 bags per year), it is not surprising that its coffees command prices around ten times that of more 'traditional' producers in Latin America and Africa.

Typica and Catuai varieties grow well and the coffee can be crisp, clean and with a pleasant winy aromatic and medium-bodied character. Many roasters offer a Kona blend, but the amount of genuine Kona in such blends can be low and they often include coffees from other origins or from lesser-quality areas of the islands. Whether pure Kona at its price is good value compared with other progressive quality-focused producers in other parts of Central America is up to the individual. At Union, we've never found enough to distinguish it from other regions or to support such prices.

Most of current production is exported to the USA, where it is enthusiastically supported as being proudly American, as well as Japan, where there seems to be little barrier to expensive imported goods with a good story. To be fair, however, the gentle acidity of this coffee is attractive to Japanese national tastes.

Jamaica

Blue Mountain is probably the world's most famous coffee name and one of the most consistently expensive. Arguably its place in the pantheon owes more to historical perspectives than to outright quality when compared with other regions today.

Established during the British colonial period in the early 1800s, coffee was produced on feudal estates that benefited from the exploitation of slave labour and beneficial trading terms with the British mainland. After these conditions came to an end in the mid-1800s, production fell rapidly and it was not until after the end of World War II that an export-oriented focus on quality (and some very clever marketing) was again driving its success. This crucially came at a time when the comparable quality of coffees from other established producing countries was not as we find today and the naturally sweet, balanced nature of Jamaica's coffee was enough to distinguish it from other offerings.

Blue Mountain refers to a very specific region of Jamaica and only coffees grown in four small sub-districts above 900m (3000ft) can be referred to as 'Jamaica Blue Mountain'. Lower-grown and lesser-quality beans can be sold as High Mountain, Supreme or Mountain coffees. However, many of these coffees are used to blend in and reduce cost. Beware any pack offering 'Blue Mountain blend' or 'Blue Mountain style' as they are highly unlikely to demonstrate the true style of this coffee and represent very poor value – especially when compared to some of the outstanding coffees of Central America.

Mexico

Most coffee produced in Mexico makes its way north to the markets of the USA; very little high-quality coffee of this origin is found in the European markets. The exceptions are the Fairtrade-led brands, as Mexico – along with Nicaragua and latterly Peru and Honduras – has used these certifications to achieve higher or more stable prices. Most coffee now grown in Mexico is under smallholder producers in the southern highlands around Veracruz, Oaxaca and Chiapas regions.

Having most likely arrived in the country from the Caribbean, the coffees show light-bodied, gently acidic profiles but without some of the complex berry fruit or floral notes of their regional competitors in El Salvador and Guatemala. The best of Mexico's coffees come from Oaxaca and Chiapas and can offer a pleasurable coffee of good clarity, much like a simple light white wine: clean with a slightly dry crisp finish.

Nicaragua

Like many countries, Nicaragua's coffee story is one of boom and bust, with a heavy overlay of political, financial and climatic causative factors. Coffee production was a significant export industry for the country following a mass planting programme that established volume production from the 1850s onwards. From the early 20th century, changes to land ownership laws saw production switch from larger estates to smallholders that until the revolution in 1979 continued to support production. Since then, the country has had a run of bad luck, culminating in 1998 when Hurricane Mitch destroyed many coffee farms and much national infrastructure, and displaced tens of thousands of farmers and workers from their land.

Fortunately, the country appears to now be in a more stable period and support for the industry is again at the forefront, with liberalized laws allowing small producers to export their own crops. This has enabled direct contact with buyers and farmers are clearly listening to what the market wants; there is world-class coffee from the districts of Jinotega, Matagalpa and Nueva Segovia. The best of these coffees have rounded medium body with juicy, fresh and clean citrus and floral notes.

Drying cherries at the Emporium Farm in Panama. Note the raised drying tables and the separate yellow and bright-red coffees. They will be processed as separate lots.

Panama

Panama's coffee is well known to consumers in the USA but until very recently has been relatively unrecognized in Europe, mainly due to its small size and output: around 100,000 bags, the smallest of any Central American country. This small-scale production, coupled with a higher cost of labour and recent demand for development, has driven land and therefore coffee prices above what the commodity-importing European trade would see as good value. Much of the country is under pressure of development, with increasing numbers of US citizens building holiday and retirement homes. The country uses the US dollar as its currency, making it more attractive still for Americans.

Historically, the best coffee-growing land was in the Boquete Valley in the north-west of the country, between the town of David and the slopes of Volcan Baru just to the north. We've always been fans of these coffees. The trees are a mixture of Bourbon and other older varietals, and in the climate of Boquete they produce intensely floral and sweet coffees with elegant layers of flavour that build complexity on the palate like a great Sauvignon Blanc wine.

In recent years, a new star has shone from Panama: the Geisha (or Gesha) variety, which is believed to have found its way to Panama from its birthplace in Ethiopia through what is still a highly contested view of history, smuggling and protected development. This variety has captivated many coffee professionals. When well produced – and not all are – it is notably distinctive in the cup, with intense jasmine floral aromas, delicate acidity and a light-bodied, super-clean character. It has also benefited from a very well orchestrated marketing campaign by one of its early advocates and producers. This is one of the highest priced coffees currently in cultivation, and although the prices will come down as more is grown, its current pricing is due to the difficulty of producing it and its low yield – which make for a significantly higher cost per hectare.

One other aspect of real note is the current trend to explore different post-harvesting methods in taking the coffee bean from the fruit through to its naked export-ready state. Many of the major developments in natural and honey processing, to produce coffees with intense fruit-driven characters, have occurred here. Some of our most characterful coffees now come from Graciano Cruz's farms in the Boquete Valley.

GRACIANO CRUZ

OWNER, EMPORIUM FARM AND LOS LAJONES FARM, BOQUETE, CHIRIQUÍ, PANAMA

Los Lajones estate has unique geological characteristics because of its position between two volcanic lava flows, which creates a specific microclimate. When Graciano Cruz and his father Graciano bought Los Lajones in 1992, the farm was used mainly for cattle pasture. The lower parts of the property were the first to be gradually planted with coffee trees. The focus then shifted to the higher section, with the Geisha variety being planted as high as 2100m (6900ft) above sea level. In 2004, Los Lajones became the first organic-certified coffee farm in Panama. Though it is no longer certified, all farm practices are 100 per cent organic and the coffee is all shade-grown. Emporium estate is a unique combination of coffee trees and hundreds of citrus trees. The workers on the farm are Ngöbe-Buglé Indians living on site.

Below: View from Emporium Farm, Panama.
Right: Graciano Cruz with freshly picked cherries.

'My great-grandfather Luis Landero was one of the first coffee farmers in Boquete. My dad mostly farmed vegetables but he always had a small coffee plantation. I grew up with coffee around me and I started farming my own coffee in 2003, although I was processing my father's coffee a year earlier. I completed a degree in Agriculture in Honduras, then studied in Nova Scotia and Japan; in 2011, I completed my MBA from INCAE, an extension of Harvard Business School for Latin America.

I base my coffee farming on bringing to coffee drinkers a new experience in tasting. I have seen the coffee industry all around the world: in Central and South America, as well as Africa and the consuming countries. It became clear to me that improving coffee quality benefits not only farmers but farm workers, too. We are lucky to be part of a time in coffee culture where there is more innovation than ever before. We are finally trying to put science into coffee, from agronomy, to post-harvesting, to roasting and brewing. Not only to increase yields or disease tolerance, but also to study the factors that create quality in the cup. And speciality coffee is paying attention to serious research in these areas.

My respect for baristas is loud and clear: these guys are the present and future of the coffee industry. Baristas are in a position to bring the real life of coffee farmers to their customers, to let consumers know how many millions of people are giving all their life for that beautiful cup of coffee that the barista just made. When I travel abroad, it is a sweet feeling to taste my coffees from a barista. It's a special connection for ever.'

SOUTH AMERICA

For the coffee lover, this is a region of vast riches and diversity, from the balanced red fruit and light red wine tones of Colombia down to Brazil with its predominantly nutty praline or maple syrup/toffee styles.

Peru and Bolivia clearly have potential, and **Ecuador** and **Venezuela** are both producing some good coffees, although very little of the best leaves the country. Venezuelan consumption just about matches national output. This was not always the case, however, and before petroleum became the major export commodity from the 1920s onwards, Venezuela was among the top five international coffee producers. But focus on the oil sector has left investment and opportunity for coffee farmers at the bottom of the government to-do list.

Main coffee-growing regions

Bolivia

At the smaller end of the league table of exporting countries (around 150,000 x 69kg bags), Bolivia was a latecomer to commercial coffee production: activities only really became established from around 1950. Even today, a fine balance exists between cultivation of coca (for the cocaine trade) and/or coffee, based on market prices. When world coffee prices fall, farmers fall back on coca production, which produces a higher income per hectare. Transport challenges (there are some seriously treacherous mountain roads) and lack of infrastructure and support for coffee farmers have prevailed against quality and have consigned Bolivia's coffee to the blending bins of large multinational brands' lower-quality blends or instant coffee production.

Since 2004, as part of a concerted effort to marginalize the crops of illegal drugs, significant international (USAID) funding has provided technical support to coffee producers in order to improve their crops. Though still rarely seen, Bolivian coffee is beginning to be more widely traded as speciality coffee.

The majority of Bolivia's quality coffee is grown in the central Yungas region, marked out by mountain ranges to the west and east that run down from the main Andes range. The best coffees from this region are grown at between 1000 and 2000m (3300–6500ft) and are produced as fully washed coffees, dried on the raised beds that were introduced as part of quality improvement programmes.

Brazil

Brazil is huge, in land area, population and coffee production and consumption: Brazilians consume around 6kg per capita, around three times as much as the UK. It is the world's largest producer, growing both Arabica and Robusta. The country produces more than a third of the world's supply, but most is considered low-grade coffee. This mass production also provides good reason to think about traceability of the coffee: the most 'famous' name of Brazil coffee exported is Santos, which is merely the major coffee exporting port – coffees designated as Santos may represent just about any quality and be from just about any farm in the country.

Production in Brazil is some of the most efficient in the world. Many coffee-growing areas are significantly less mountainous than those in Central America, and coffee is grown on large expanses of hillside and plateau at altitudes ranging from 600 to 1100m (2000–3600ft). The flat terrain, coupled with the economic strength of the country, has stimulated the formation of very large estates, where mechanization and volume are key. Coffees are picked by harvesting machines and processed in vast mills where the entire process is handled, from cherry to export-ready green coffee. The professionalism of these estates is to be respected as they produce qualities that are well above commodity, but which can never achieve the greatness of well-managed small farm production. But there is excellent coffee in Brazil, a country of over 200,000 producers. Our Union Direct Trade approach has allowed us to find exceptional coffee here. In a country where heavy chemical use and spraying is the norm we work with the Croce family at a farm called Fazenda Ambiental Fortaleza, 10 per cent of whose coffee is certified organic, all of it being hand-picked and processed with care.

Most of Brazil's quality coffee comes from the vast states of São Paulo and Minas Gerais on the south-eastern side of the country. The climate there is wetter and milder than the drier north, where mass irrigation systems are required to support coffee production.

Brazil has been a haven for the original Bourbon variety first introduced in the early 18th century. Bourbon, along with newer Brazilian varieties such as Mundo Novo and Icatu, is responsible for the milk-chocolate/praline-smooth character, low acidity and full body that makes Brazilian coffees so versatile for espresso as well as filter coffee brewing. Brazil coffees are pretty evenly split between washed, natural and the pulped natural (honey) process.

Below left: In Colombia old fertilizer sacks are often used to carry parchment coffee. The colourful sacks below are produced specifically as a clean alternative. Below right: Local chiva bus used to transport people, goods and chickens.

Colombia

Colombia is the world's third largest producer, after Brazil and Vietnam, and one of the oldest in South America: beans were planted there in the 18th century and commercial production was established by the 1830s. Coffee has been the country's most important (legal) export crop since the mid-19th century, and while large farms have historically dominated other areas of agriculture, smaller farms have long been a major feature of coffee production.

Since 1927 coffee producers have been supported by the Federación Nacional de Cafeteros or FNC (National Federation of Coffee Growers), which uses an export levy on all coffee sold to provide assistance in areas from agronomy and finance through to export marketing. It's this latter area that makes the FNC unique as a producer organization. Its vision of making Colombian coffee 'the world's most famous coffee' came through the marketing efforts of Juan Valdez, a fictional coffee grower used in

Peru

advertising worldwide. The concept was that all Colombian coffee is excellent (a commonly held view that many producing countries have of their own crop) and that only two designations need be created: Excelso and Supremo. These are simply different sizes of bean – Excelso the smaller and Supremo the larger – and neither term refers in any way to quality.

All coffee, to enable the continued funding of the increasingly powerful FNC, had to be sold through its system. This inevitably led to the commoditization of its coffee, with huge tranches of average quality swallowing up outstanding smaller parcels. The result was inevitably mediocre, and almost destroyed the availability of speciality-grade, fully traceable coffee.

But as Colombia seeks to play catch-up with other countries that have exploited regionality, export laws have been liberalized and today it is possible for individual cooperatives and growers' associations to export their coffee directly.

The main producing areas are sometimes called the 'coffee triangle'. The region is now recognized as a UNESCO World Heritage area under the name Paisaje Cultural Cafetero (Coffee Cultural Landscape of Colombia). We work with two producers, Asprotimana Cooperative in Huila and Finca Santuario in Valle de Cauca.

Coffees from Colombia range from delicate lightly fruity coffees through to a fuller-bodied jammy style with a red-wine-like finish. The best coffees are always noted for their balance of sweetness and medium acidity.

As in many Central and South American countries, coffee production in Peru faced significant challenges over the 20th century, with politics and conflict causing a lack of development, investment and international marketing efforts. By the early 1980s production was significantly reduced and farmers received prices that were barely above international market rates, with most coffee sold for mass-market blends.

But then Peru, after Nicaragua, became one of the first countries to benefit from 'cause-related marketing', most notably the beginning of the Fairtrade movement which established a base floor price above that of the markets (for cooperatives but not family-owned single farm enterprises). The average coffee producer is a smallholder with a farm of less than 5 hectares (about 12 acres). Therefore, many producers market their coffee through a cooperative.

Peru has also been at the forefront of organic-certified coffee production and this too has helped drive interest and hence premiums from roasters. Disappointingly, it has appeared that the increased costs of production are not always covered by the market price.

We are very fortunate to have worked since 2009 with Chirinos Cooperative in the southern Cajamarca region, which does a tremendous amount of good work on quality control to provide us with the highest-quality coffees from their harvest.

Peru has without doubt unlimited potential to grow superior coffees. The traditional varieties that produce exceptional coffee, such as Typica and Bourbon, are grown in the high mountainous areas, sometimes at altitudes greater than 2000m (6500ft). Unfortunately, these coffees are often poorly picked and processed and finding real gems is not easy.

THE ECONOMY OF COFFEE

Many people have images of coffee farming in their minds. For some it's about beautiful mountains, old estate plantation houses and cloud forests, for others the image is one of rural poverty and mud huts. In an industry where worldwide some 125 million people gain their income from coffee farming, both are true. Many coffee producers do it as an accident of birth, and many are lucky to make a sustainable income.

Given that coffee is among the most widely traded commodities, and given our insatiable habit for the brew, why are so many farmers so badly affected? One of the prime reasons is that coffee is traded as a commodity and its market price day to day has nothing to do with its quality. It is more about the balance of supply and demand, and increasingly about the next upcoming drought, frost or even over-supply as investor funds look for strength or weakness in global markets, be they coffee, cocoa, oil, wheat or steel.

The coffee world looks daily to the New York Board of Trade (NYBOT), the exchange where prices are set against defined contract periods. The market price is referred to as the C-contract price – or simply the C-price – and in reality very few of the paper notes that pass across the exchange are for actual containers of sacks filled with fresh green coffee beans. They are traded on the basis that the price and hence the contract value will be higher tomorrow and a profit can be banked for the trading houses, banks and hedge funds. Complex options and hedging mechanisms designed to offset losses add to this swirl of financial activity.

This casino approach causes huge instability for farmers as they depend on knowing how much they can make from their single crop – remember, many coffee farmers do not have any other cash crop and

depend upon their harvest for the household budget. In addition the market effect has largely flattened the price that farmers receive over time and the C-price today, barring short-term upswings and downturns, remains broadly the same as it was 30 years ago.

The premium proposition

While the international market sets the base price, it is common for many countries to receive premiums above this. The higher the reputation or demand for a country, region or even specific producer, the higher these premiums can be. When markets are lower they provide a life-saving top-up – but they rarely come much above the cost of production, leaving little profit for the farmer.

Even in times of good prices, such is the nature of global connectedness through mobile phones that everyone (including pickers, truck drivers and mill workers) knows the price is up and will expect higher wages. The farmer who has to contract all of these services sits last in the line.

Our personal challenge over the years since starting Union has been to unpick all of these parts and processes and to recognize and value each stage in the supply chain so that the price the farmer receives is a fair and sustainable one for growing coffee. From our own observation, we believe that the true cost of production for high-quality coffee is around 20 per cent higher than the Fairtrade minimum price of $1.40. (The cost for commodity-grade coffee is lower.) What we have in common with Fairtrade is a commitment to making sure farmers are not at the mercy of the international commodity markets.

Below: All forms of transport (including human) are used to deliver parchment coffee to the warehouse.

The coffee cycle

Coffee takes a very long time to get from the farm to your breakfast table. A huge number of people are involved all the way along the supply chain. All of them require payment. The following is not intended to be an accurate calendar, but it illustrates the life cycle of a single crop. As can be seen in this many-handed chain, by the time the farmer receives payment for the crop, preparations for the following year are already under way.

③ **FEBRUARY**

① **MAY**

The coffee trees begin to flower. Nine months then pass while the flowers develop into fruit. Constant light work around the farm is essential: trees need to be maintained and the ground kept clear of weeds. Heavy rain can cause flowers and fruit to be lost.

The majority of coffee cherries are ripening and it's time to start picking. Paying pickers is around 60 per cent of the annual cost of producing coffee.

⑤ **APRIL**

Tail end of the harvest. All fruit must be picked, as rotting fruit on the trees can attract pests that cause damage to the trees or to next year's crop. Trees are pruned and fertilized ready for the next flowering.

② **JANUARY**

Coffee cherries are still developing. With too much or too little rain or sun, cherries can fail to mature or to develop their sugars and the final quality will be lower.

④ **MARCH**

Peak harvest season and long working hours for farmers who process their own cherries. Picking by day and depulping and washing by night places a high demand on families. Farmers in a cooperative might deliver their cherries to a central washing or processing station instead of processing at home. They will receive a lower price but with a second payment due on export.

⑥ APRIL–MAY

Once the harvest is complete, any farm or cooperative that exports their coffee direct must look at the smaller batches and work out how to compile exportable parcels of coffee. These need to bulk up into shipping container quantities of between 275 and 300 sacks. In the case of average-quality coffees traded by larger exporters, this work is done by the export house and the bulk lots will be blended from many farms to produce a regional or merely country-level style. For the quality-focused producer, samples of daily production are roasted, cupped and evaluated. In smallholder communities this may be just a few sacks, so a great many lots need to be sampled and assessed so that the flavour characteristics of the final lot represent the character and quality expected by the buyers.

⑧ JULY

The coffee is milled from its parchment layer. The milling is done by an external company and the cost of this may come out of the farmer's or producer's pocket either directly or as a reduction in the price paid by the exporter. In addition, at this stage any physical defects or damage arising during growing, harvesting, drying and milling become apparent and it may be necessary to remove a small percentage of the crop in order to protect the cup quality. Again, the farmer often pays for this.

The milled coffee, now in its hessian or jute bags (weighing 69kg or 60kg depending on country of origin), is loaded into the container to go on board the ship. Once on board, the export documents are presented to the buyer for payment to be arranged. Payment is then made to either exporter or cooperative and the work that began in April the previous year can finally be converted to cash.

⑦ MAY–JUNE

The current crop is now 'resting', still inside its dried papery skin, or parchment. During this period, the coffee can be marketed. Samples of exportable lots ('offer samples') are sent out from the export companies to buyers around the world – usually importers, sometimes roasters, who in turn roast, taste and assess them for their own businesses and markets. When an agreement to buy has been made, a contract is written specifying delivery date, price and quality characteristics to be observed and the coffee can finally be prepared for its journey.

SINGLE FARMER COMPARED TO COOPERATIVE FARMER

If a small farmer operates alone, rather than as part of a cooperative or association that can export coffee in volume, he or she will often sell to a local collector who gathers in coffee on behalf of a larger exporter. Depending upon the nature of that relationship, the farmer might not get paid until the coffee is sold on the international market some weeks or even months later.

Members of a cooperative may receive an immediate payment ('first payment') – a lower price than the commercial market rate so as not to overburden the cooperative with high upfront costs. Once the coffee is sold the cooperative then calculates the profit and distributes this as a second payment to the member farmers.

WEIGHT/VALUE CHANGES THROUGH THE PROCESS

The fruit pulp makes up a significant proportion of the overall weight of the coffee cherry. For every 100kg of cherries picked, after depulping this yields around 20kg of beans with mucilage and parchment. After sun-drying and removal of the parchment layer, around 8kg of beans remains; and after further quality grading, there may be a net yield of 7.2kg of green coffee sold.

The final change in weight/value comes at the roasting stage, where around 15–20 per cent of the green coffee mass is lost. So 100kg of coffee cherries picked from the tree ends up as 5.7kg of roasted coffee.

The share of income is complicated by this multi-stage weight loss through the value chain. Statements made by some advocacy groups about the price per kilo that farmers receive can be highly misleading – but can make good headlines.

THE SKILL OF CUPPING AND GETTING A GOOD PRICE

A natural outcome in farming is that from the entire harvest a small quantity (around 5–10 per cent) may be of a very top grade, with around 60–80 per cent being 'market acceptable' and the rest only suitable for 'local consumption', i.e. not worth exporting. Traditionally, all the coffee over local grade is sold together, but more and more producers are looking at optimizing their crops by choosing the best customer and thereby getting the best possible prices. Any producer group with a skilled in-house or local cupper can benefit from feedback and advice on quality, helping farmers to recognize and segregate the higher-quality lots. These separated parcels are often referred to as micro-lots and can achieve prices above that of the 'standard' crop.

With the rise of certification schemes that do not require any statement of quality, incomes can be managed by selling the 'standard' lots through these channels and a minimal income level is boosted.

The cupping table at RWASHOSCCO, Kigali; ready to assess the character and quality of different Rwanda coffees.

ETHICAL TRADING

Much is said nowadays about ethical sourcing of food and drink. The term has no legal definition, so it is one to be treated with some caution. We are not commenting on any other company's policies here, but our requirements in this area can serve as a useful discussion of what you should look for in deciding where to buy your coffee.

An early direct relationship at Union was with Huila, Colombia, where we supported a quality lab and training for local cuppers of Asprotimana Cooperative.

Union Direct Trade

The global price for commodity coffee is the C-contract price (usually known as the C-price), which refers to the price being traded on the New York Board of Trade commodity futures exchange. Commodity coffee, by definition, has no intrinsic value – which means that quality is not rewarded. The mainstream coffee market, which trades commodity-grade coffee, can be viewed as an adversarial system. There is no relationship or loyalty between farmer and buyer (often a trading company), so the buyer can seek a coffee from a different country or producer, in order to pay the lowest price. The C-price does not take account of the production costs of coffee. This inhibits the farmer from achieving any business stability, planning for their future or investing in their farm. And when the C-price is low the impact can spell disaster for coffee-producing communities.

This economic model has not worked for coffee farmers: ethical trading makes an attempt to redress the balance.

In our desire to create an alternative trading approach, we developed our coffee-sourcing initiative called Union Direct Trade. This gives us access to high-quality speciality coffee while also improving the livelihoods of coffee farmers.

Through Union Direct Trade, we source our coffee from developing countries, establishing long-term commercial relationships with small-scale farmers and their workers. For the coffee farmers it provides incentive and inspiration to improve the quality of their coffee, aided by regular active support from us. By creating access to speciality markets we enable producers to improve their income, and we have seen how our approach to sustainable trade has changed the lives of hundreds, probably thousands, of coffee farmers and their families.

Following the principles of development economics, we view Union Direct Trade as an inclusive business model. Which means we are a for-profit sustainable business that benefits low-income coffee-farming communities which are so important in our coffee supply. This is not just corporate social responsibility, it is our heart and soul. The core principles of Union Direct Trade are:

Quality of coffee

- We source 100 per cent high-quality, high-altitude-grown speciality Arabica coffee.
- We agree a quality price incentive with producers, which means we select outstanding coffee, scoring more than 84 points (out of 100) on the SCAA scale.
- We pay an additional premium for exemplary quality, scoring 88+ on the SCAA scale.

Quality of life

- Fair working conditions, guaranteed by the producer's commitment to the Union code of conduct for ethical sourcing.
- Union-led social audits of working conditions on farms that employ permanent and seasonal workers.
- Sustainable pricing: our base price is 25 per cent above the Fairtrade minimum price, and is further enhanced through quality premiums.
- Price verification: financial transparency throughout the supply chain is verified by visits and social audit inspections.

Quality of business (good purchasing practices)

- Transparent financial transactions with all participants in the supply chain, which includes facilities at wet mills, dry mills and specialized export services.
- Commitment to develop long-term relationships extending to multi-year purchases. Nearly 70 per cent of our coffee is sourced from producers we've been working with for more than six years.
- Supporting access to credit at the beginning of the season when producers are most in need.

We develop and maintain relationships with farmers through active involvement: we visit producers 'in the field' every 12–24 months to monitor quality, provide feedback and discuss business goals. We encourage producers to spread risk by negotiating a maximum of 50 per cent of our suppliers' crop before the harvest, to avoid mutual dependence. Minimum volumes are always established before the harvest, which allows farmers to plan ahead. We offer sustainable prices and a buyer who stands with them year after year; this long-term security gives farmers the confidence to invest in their coffee lands. We cherish these relationships, yet we make demands to always aspire to better quality.

Top left: Union producer relationships manager, Pascale Schuit, with children of Esquipulas Cooperative, Guatemala – she's the one with the butterfly mask. Top right: Jeremy with the women of Maraba, Rwanda, at the drying tables. Centre: Jeremy at the entrance to Union's third cooperative, Koakaka Cooperative, Karaba, Rwanda. Bottom left: Steven at the worm farm used for composting pulped cherries, Maraba, Rwanda. Bottom right: In 2015 Union took producer Graciano Cruz from Panama to run farmer workshops on quality in Yayu, Ethiopia.

Ethical Trading Initiative: respect for workers worldwide

Our Union code of conduct is founded on the conventions of the International Labour Organization (ILO), and is an internationally recognized code of labour practice. We created this through our membership of the Ethical Trading Initiative (ETI), which is a tripartite organization: membership is comprised of Trade Unions, Non-Government Organizations and companies all working together to improve labour standards throughout the supply chain (ethicaltrade.org).

Ethical Trading Initiative promotes the improvement of standards by following strict principles: employment must be freely chosen, collective bargaining is allowed, pay must be fair, working conditions must be safe and hygienic, work must be regular and hours not excessive, child labour will not be used, no discrimination is practised, and no harsh or inhumane treatment is allowed.

Direct trade

The general term 'direct trade' is now often used to indicate that the roaster has bought the coffee directly from the farmer, and implies that no other participants such as exporters or importers are involved. To be genuinely worthwhile the roaster has to buy enough coffee from a producer to have a financial impact, and also have the resources to verify financial transparency throughout the supply chain. Direct trade is not solely concerned with going to origin, cupping and selecting the best-tasting coffee. The ideal is a sustainable approach that develops long-term relationships with farmers and supports them financially as well as through knowledge-sharing to produce the best quality coffees.

Pascale Schuit, Union's manager of producer relationships, taking a bus to a training workshop with producers from Todos Santos, Huehuetenango, Guatemala.

FINCA CANDELARIA

GUATEMALA

We buy from a very special farm called Finca Candelaria, which has a stunning view towards two volcanoes, Acatenango and Fuego. It is one of the few larger farms we source from, extending to around 200 hectares (500 acres). Fourth-generation coffee producer, miller and exporter Luis Pedro Zelaya has a background in agronomy. He owns and manages several farms, including one called Bella Vista where all the post-harvest operations (fermenting, washing, drying and hulling the coffees picked from other farms) are carried out.

Luis Pedro Zelaya takes care of his soils and ensures his plants are healthy using environmentally friendly practices: organic material (mulch) decomposes and fertilizes the coffee plants. Biological pest and disease control is practised against the coffee berry borer, a small beetle that attacks the fruit. Instead of treating the coffee trees with insecticides, the insect is controlled using traps filled with a substance that attracts them. These traps have proven very successful in Latin America.

Above: Luis Pedro Zelaya (right) and his father, also Luis Pedro. Left: The stunning location of Finca Candelaria.

Fairtrade

Most of the world's coffee is roasted and packed by multinationals whose profit motive drives purchasing to a lowest-cost route. They blend coffee to yield a 'market-acceptable' product as opposed to one that stimulates consumers' interest. This has maintained a buyer's market, with farmers having to take or leave the price offers put to them. Unfortunately, as production costs have increased over the years, the market price has not rewarded them. In times of unusually low prices, many have lost their land or had to move out of coffee and into other local traded crops, preserving a smallholder subsistence economy.

Fairtrade certification set the tone for a new approach that would fulfil the need for socially sustainable coffee production by providing a price safety net. The system works by guaranteeing that the exporter of the coffee pays the cooperative at least the Fairtrade Minimum Price and Fairtrade Premium; reasonable deductions may be made for expenses such as processing and logistical support. There is a further premium for organic coffee that pays 30 cents per pound above the Fairtrade floor price, but it is arguable whether this really covers the lower yields and hence increased cost of organic production.

There is no doubt that Fairtrade has achieved real benefits for some farmers and cooperatives, and has played an important part in raising consumer awareness of the issue of rewarding producers for their labour. Some Fairtrade coffees are very good, but consumers should not automatically equate Fairtrade with high quality.

When market prices are very low, all farmers receive the same price for their crops, regardless of cup quality. And quality does not feature among the criteria for becoming certified: only social structures, management controls and (in recent years) environmental standards are examined. Much Fairtrade-certified production has therefore remained mass-market commodity-grade coffee, which doesn't always change producers' lives in a significant way. There is no built-in incentive for the individual farmer to focus on quality or innovation. If they want to earn more money, they have to grow more coffee. There is already an oversupply of Fairtrade certified coffee, so we would say the better approach is: don't grow more, grow better. If you improve the quality of your coffee and find the right market for it, you will achieve the same aims (at least) that Fairtrade has admirably set out to promote.

Fairtrade is a systematized and transparent way to conduct trade, and that is obviously a good thing. But no farmer wants you to buy their coffee because they're labelled as 'poor'. A long-term relationship, season after season, works both ways between buyer and producer. This undoubtedly happens sometimes under Fairtrade, and we support their general aims. We simply take a different approach to achieving them, focusing on coffee of the highest possible quality. This, we believe, is the best way to manage the coffee supply chain. It's more difficult to explain than buying a pack of coffee with a succinct logo, but it's more effective for the farmer and more pleasurable for the customer.

Other social trading models

Rainforest Alliance grew out of an environmental advocacy group. Initially weak on social aspects, the code has improved in recent years. Unlike Fairtrade, it does not set a minimum price obligation upon the buyers. Rainforest Alliance also makes it easier (cheaper) for big brands to gain certification, because products only have to contain a smaller (but steadily rising) certified content.

Other certification marks are seen in various countries. Utz is a Netherlands-based label for sustainable farming. Bird Friendly – operated by the Smithsonian Institution in the USA – guarantees organic farming.

Jeremy judging at the Cup of Excellence competition in Colombia, 2010. Union regularly participates as volunteer judges at international quality competitions. At the Cup of Excellence competition around 50 of the top coffees are judged over five days to find the best of the country's harvest that year.

CUP OF EXCELLENCE

The year 1999 saw the first Cup of Excellence competition, run as a non-profit venture to encourage producers to raise their quality, and choose particularly good lots to sell separately as micro-lots rather than selling their coffees at market price for blending. The incentive to take part came from an internet auction at the end of the competition, when the winning beans would be sold on the open market – and at prices that far exceeded those established daily on the commodity-trading market.

Today the Cup of Excellence is run in ten countries and receives thousands of entrants every year. The competition lasts three weeks, with international judges in the final stage. The organization behind Cup of Excellence is the Alliance for Coffee Excellence (ACE), based in Portland, Oregon.

Many independent roasters take every opportunity to buy Cup of Excellence coffees, and we are among them. Indeed, we regard ourselves as lucky to get them. But the top award-winners are always very expensive. In 2015 we purchased a parcel of Bella Vista Cup of Excellence No 1, grown in Colombia. We were crazy about it. But because of the high price we had paid at auction, we had to sell it for £20.50 for 125g. By way of comparison: another lovely Colombia of ours, Finca Santuario, was selling for £28.50 *per kilo*.

The Cup of Excellence is a way to make sure that coffees of truly exceptional quality find their way to market without being blended. The only way to do that is by paying the producers – who do get most of the money, by the way – prices that will make the effort worthwhile for them. And there are knock-on effects as well. Thinking about entering the competition will in itself make producers try to improve the quality of what they grow. And even if they don't win the top prize, runners-up are included in the auctions and can expect to sell their best lots for a substantial premium.

ORGANIC COFFEE

Organic coffee is grown using methods that have a low impact on the environment. Organic production systems try to maintain soil fertility, avoid erosion and build healthy ecosystems.

To control insects on organic farms, traps such as these are used. Made from old plastic bottles, a fruit juice solution is placed inside to attract insects that then drown inside.

A farm that calls itself organic has to be certified as such by an accredited inspection agency. Farmers cannot use synthetic fertilizers. Instead, they should choose organic fertilizer options such as animal manure, coffee pulp or general compost. Farmers cannot use pesticides, fungicides or herbicides to prevent or combat diseases such as leaf rust. Instead they should apply 'integrated pest and disease management' which means that by proper fertilizing, pruning and building a healthy environment the farmer creates an ecosystem that is less vulnerable to attack from pest and disease. But if a plantation is affected by pests there is no quick solution. Organic farmers also take great care of their farm by growing shade trees (which promote a natural ecosystem), weeding manually and keeping the soil fertile with organic nutrient material. Growing organic coffee can be a complex strategy.

If organic production means no expensive chemical inputs, does this make it cheaper than conventional farming? Almost every organic coffee farmer will argue that it is more expensive. Cenicafé, a leading coffee research centre, reported that 12kg of composted coffee pulp is equivalent to 150g of synthetic fertilizer. This is the amount required per tree each year. Multiply that for 4000 trees planted in a hectare and you will see that makes a difference of 47,400kg of fertilizer that needs to be transported, moved and placed around the trees. Extra transport and extra labour cost a lot of extra money.

Farmers will also tell you that organic coffee farming is more labour-intensive. Using one worker with a backpack sprayer, a hectare of coffee can be treated with herbicides to clear weeds in one day. But you would need four or six workers to clear that same hectare manually. In some countries wages are as low as $5 a day, whereas in other coffee-producing countries, such as Brazil, wages may be $60 a day. So in many circumstances organic coffee production is more expensive than conventional production.

And then there is the organic certification fee, which is somewhere around US$3000–4000 a year. Some of the producers we work with could get their farms certified, but choose not to, partly or largely for reasons of cost.

ORGANIC BY DEFAULT

Very few small-scale coffee farmers apply pesticides to their trees. In 2011 we asked 90 Guatemalan farmers about pesticide use and only 3 per cent indicated they use them. Many producers are 'organic by default', which actually means they lack the financial resources to invest in farm inputs. This often is not the optimal situation for the farmer, because although not using fertilizer or pesticides saves money, the quality and the quantity of the coffee yield will be reduced. An investment in fertilizer (either organic or non-organic) will pay off because the farmer will harvest more coffee. But in countries with high levels of poverty, making an investment today to reap the fruits in a couple of months is a difficult decision.

WHY DO FARMERS OPT TO GROW ORGANIC?

Farmers we source from who grow according to organic systems are motivated by the philosophical principles of organic production. They feel a responsibility towards the environment and the maintenance of soil, trees and healthy biodiversity on the farm. These farmers tell us that organic production is a way of living and they take on the responsibility to protect nature.

Steven at the entrance to our friends Silvio and Celso's small farm in São Paolo State, Brazil.

ROASTING

In the world of food and drink, there can be few things that come anywhere near the almost magical transformation that coffee undergoes in its roasting. Coffee roasting is a creative art, the alchemy of changing green seeds with almost no flavour into chestnut-brown beans that release an intoxicatingly heady aroma.

This is the world of the coffee roaster. We select fine coffees from many countries, each capable of producing a different cup, and by working with different timings and temperatures arrive at a final roast that presents the coffee in its best light. It's a constantly changing and challenging world: throughout the year after harvest, the green coffee can change ever so slightly and the roast will need to be modified to take account of these changes.

In large companies, roasting is often done by technicians who manage computerized plants; they make no decision as to how the coffee should taste, they just follow the flight plan. For those of us at the small end of this trade, choosing to work with higher-quality speciality grade coffees, roasting is a long way from mere processing. Understanding what has gone into producing the finished green beans, we feel a personal responsibility to make the most of those beans through roasting.

The description of roasting that follows is based on our practice, developed over years in our own company. We are not saying it is the only way of practising this intricate art, it is just the way we do it.

THE PRINCIPLES OF ROASTING

Roasting, even more than country of origin and processing method, is probably the most important aspect of coffee when it comes to flavour in the cup. At its most basic level, roasting is responsible for the perception of 'strength'. Light roasts will be perceived as lighter in body and bright on the palate. Darker roasts feel heavier and more intense, and as darkness increases, more bitter-sweet. The darkest roasts have a distinct smokiness and an overtly bitter character.

A good analogy here is chocolate. Imagine tasting chocolate bars from milk through dark, all the way through 75 and up to 90 or 100 per cent cocoa content. At the higher cocoa content, the fruitiness and depth of flavour of the chocolate closes down, becoming almost too intense to find flavours other than bitterness.

But roasting is much more complicated than a simple question of light versus dark. Our challenge as coffee roasters is to achieve balance through understanding the progression of the coffee throughout the roast, what we call its *development*.

How flavours change
THE DEVELOPMENT OF FLAVOUR DURING ROASTING

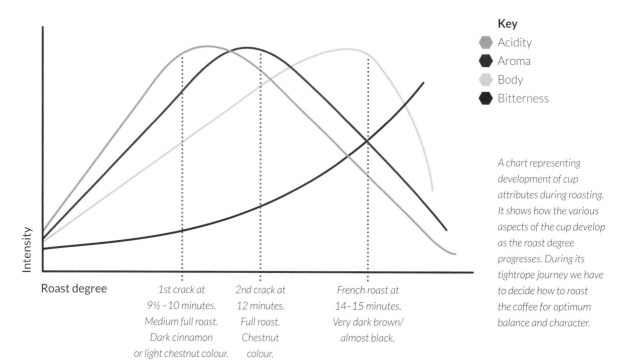

Key
- Acidity
- Aroma
- Body
- Bitterness

Intensity

Roast degree

1st crack at 9½ – 10 minutes. Medium full roast. Dark cinnamon or light chestnut colour.

2nd crack at 12 minutes. Full roast. Chestnut colour.

French roast at 14–15 minutes. Very dark brown/ almost black.

A chart representing development of cup attributes during roasting. It shows how the various aspects of the cup develop as the roast degree progresses. During its tightrope journey we have to decide how to roast the coffee for optimum balance and character.

Roaster James preparing a batch of green beans for roasting.

Two key components found in green coffee beans constitute the roaster's tightrope: sugars and naturally occurring fruit acids. These two families of compounds need almost opposite treatment during the roast. **Sugars** in their mostly natural state taste sweeter than the caramelized sugars that are created the further (darker) we go into the roast. The **acids**, particularly chlorogenic acids (CGA), begin their journey largely as phenolic, bitter or astringent flavours on the palate and need time and energy to break down into more acceptable notes. But at low levels they add to coffee's desirable characters. Successfully walking the tightrope means pushing the roast far enough for adequate breakdown of undesirable acids while preserving the sweeter sugars and balancing these two characteristics.

It's the roaster's choice as to how far to take the coffee, and a wide range of opinion exists as to what constitutes under- or over-roasting. At its worst, under-roasted coffee, where the chlorogenic acids have not broken down enough, will have sour or grassy, vegetal or phenolic notes that either taste bad or can make the cup astringent on the palate even though it may be very sweet to taste. Over-roasted coffees will be perceived as 'stronger', but this comes at a cost of being markedly less sweet with overtones of smoky caramel or very dark cocoa: a flat cup more or less devoid of the graceful acids.

When we first started roasting coffee back in the 1990s, we chose to roast dark, our inspiration having been Peet's Coffee in the San Francisco Bay area. Peet's taught us that it was possible to produce dark-roasted coffees that were still very sweet.

Over the years, however, as we've built our own network of outstanding farmers, improvements in quality have given us green coffees showing wonderful characteristics that beg to be allowed their day in the sunshine. Even with very skilful dark roasting, some of these aspects will be lost. So the majority of our coffees nowadays can be considered medium roasts – although we prefer the term 'signature roast': each coffee balances sweetness with an elegant combination of acids that allow the cup to sparkle on the palate.

The exact point at which to stop the roast is determined by agreeing exactly what shade of brown best showcases this particular batch of beans. As the roast progresses these colour changes happen more quickly. Our roasters check bean colour and aromas infrequently at first, but then stand fixed in front of the machine, constantly checking. Ten or 20 seconds can be the difference between that perfect score and 'close but no cigar'. The coffee won't be bad, but 'not bad' is not what we are aiming for.

THE ROASTING PROCESS

At Union we work with many single-origin coffees, grown at a range of altitudes, with different bean densities and of a multitude of varieties, and crafted through various techniques of post-harvest processing. Add to this the local weather and ambient temperature at the Union roastery, and our roasting crew are presented with a series of questions when approaching our daily production roasts.

When we bring a sack of beans into our roastery, we roast samples using up to six different roast profiles (time versus temperature). Then we cup all the variations to select the most delicious roast. This becomes our production roast and is passed to our roasting crew to bring to life on our vintage Probat drum roasters. These use the traditional method of slow roasting, where the drum is heated directly by flames to its outer wall.

We use computer software to log data, but the roasters are not automated or computer controlled. All our coffees are roasted by hand – watching the physical changes in the coffee and sampling, using skill to craft the profile – supported by technology as we observe the roast profile we're creating on a screen by the roaster. This is how we produce flavour and consistency in our coffee. (Other speciality roasters would probably say exactly the same thing.)

Throughout the roast progression, our roasting team are continuously anticipating what the coffee is *going* to be doing, as well as what the beans are actually doing at that moment. Our roasters are always looking ahead, using the rate of temperature change to predict what will happen later in the roast. We're acting ahead of what the beans are actually doing, making decisions about adjusting the flame, dialling down the heat or adding slight increases of gas if anticipating the roast needs greater energy. As well as checking consistency of roast on computer software, we cup each roast and this may indicate that we need to adjust the profile.

A question of density

The density of the green coffee beans affects the amount of heat needed to roast them evenly. Different varieties of coffee tree give subtly different densities, but the major factor is the altitude at which the coffee is grown: the higher the altitude, the denser the bean. It's reasonable to expect that high-grown coffees such as those from Central America will need a more pushy approach, whereas coffees from Indonesia or Brazil, where lower altitudes are more common, require a gentler hand.

For higher-grown coffees, we may choose to preheat the roaster to a higher initial temperature (the 'charge temperature') and keep our foot on the gas, so to speak, burners roaring, and when the coffee has picked up pace to gently slow things down. Lower-density coffees could by contrast benefit from a lower charge temperature and a less aggressive push on the gas. Both coffees will, however, roast in approximately the same time assuming we are seeking the same degree of darkness.

We never blend beans of different densities before roasting. Imagine trying to roast a joint of meat and bake a sponge cake in the same oven for the same length of time: one would be undercooked, the other in flames!

ROASTING MACHINES

Most quality coffee is roasted in drum roasters, in which the beans are tumbled inside a large cast-iron drum with gas burners that play their flames onto its outer wall. While the drum provides radiant heat to the beans inside, fans pull hot air through, heating the beans by convection. The combination of radiant and convected heat allows for a slow steady roast. The smallest commercial machines have batch sizes of 3–15kg, the largest up to 500kg or 1000kg.

Roasting systems used by the large multinational companies use high volumes of hot air blasted at the beans. Roasting is done very quickly, in as little as 90 seconds. In the case of the fastest roasters, speed is achieved at the expense of quality, but for low-quality and instant coffees, the development of the beans can probably be deemed adequate.

At Union we only use drum roasters, the smallest being our 100g sample roaster. Our 12kg 'San Franciscan' is used for developing roast profiles and for our roast-to-order service for home consumers. Most of our daily needs are met by two vintage Probat 120kg drum roasters. These machines are both well over 50 years old and have been lovingly restored. They give our roasts slow, steady development, and we believe that they are a key part of our success: they are not run by a computer – each batch is hand-roasted.

Top: Steve running batches on our main production roaster, a vintage 120kg drum roaster. Below left: Sight window and temperature probe on our small batch machine. We can see the colour and read off the temperature to determine how quickly the roast is developing. Below right: Lee discharging finished beans from our small roaster into the cooling tray – 10kg of perfection!

Roasting process

1

GREEN BEANS

These contain around 12 per cent moisture and vary in density between different origins. The density will determine how intense or gentle we need to be with the temperature profile of the roast.

4

EARLY DEVELOPMENT

Once the first colour change has been reached, we reduce the heat input and the beans start to expand, releasing sweet hay and bread-like aromas and producing steam. During this stage the beans flake off the chaff (silverskin), which is collected and removed.

By the time the temperature reaches 125–150°C (260–300°F), in 6–7 minutes, the Maillard reaction is under way. This reaction between sugars and proteins, which also occurs in baking bread and roasting nuts, is one of the most important in creating coffee flavour, aromas and colour. As the temperature nears 170°C (325°F), in another 2 minutes or so, natural sugars caramelize and brown.

2–3

COLOUR CHANGE

As heat energy is transferred to the bean, a sequence of reactions takes place. To get this started quickly we use a lot of power, with the flame set high, so the temperature starts rising (after dropping when the beans go in) after 1–2 minutes. It's important to get the starting temperature right: it must be hot enough to keep the roast progressing at the right rate; too cool a start and too low a flame causes the roast to 'stall', meaning that it fails to increase in temperature, which adversely affects the resulting flavours. In the first 4–6 minutes the colour changes from green to yellow as plant chlorophyll breaks down and most of the remaining moisture is driven off.

5–6

FIRST CRACK

After another 3–4 minutes, around 10–11 minutes into the roast, the release of water vapour and carbon dioxide pressure rupture the cell structure of the bean, and this makes cracking (popping) noises. Wisps of smoke and steam rise from the coffee. After first crack, the temperature can rise rapidly. A gradual increase of temperature within the drum is essential and it takes a lot of experience to achieve it. A roller-coaster roast, where temperatures rise, dip, or stall, can often result in a salty, flat and flavourless cup. Our roasters constantly watch the coffee,

PROGRESSION OF THE ROAST

1 Green   2 Green dried   3 First colour change   4 Early development

7

CONTINUED DEVELOPMENT

After first crack, carbon dioxide again builds within the bean and browning continues along with further breakdown of sugars. Coffees between first and second crack become less sweet and more 'roasty' in flavour but fuller in body. If continuing further, temperature must be controlled so as not to end too high too soon, when either flames or an ashy taste will result.

SECOND CRACK

After the first crack subsides the temperature will again, if left unchecked, begin to rise at a faster rate. Again an adjustment to the flame is made to allow things to progress gently. Airflow through the roaster is important throughout the roast but particularly in the late stages, when considerable volumes of blue smoke are produced. If not vented out, the coffee will develop an over-smoky taste in the cup.

Over the following 1–3 minutes, carbon dioxide continues to build up, forcing a minute spot of oil to the surface of the bean. The second crack (pop) is under way. It takes nerve and expertise to correctly roast into second crack: roasting to this degree is near the ignition temperature of the bean. Regular cleaning of ducting and pipework means that roaster fires are very rare.

and use their senses to detect the point at which the aromas are super-sweet and bread-like. Today, most of the coffees we roast at Union are finished shortly after the first crack. The acids are broken down to a point where their better-tasting by-products dominate and support the other complex aromatics and flavour compounds, and sweetness is retained.

FRENCH ROAST

This is the darkest roast and is rarely offered for quality coffees as the predominant taste is that of carbonization (burnt toast), with all of the elemental flavours of the beans themselves already burnt off or degraded. The coffee, if not too dark, will have very full body (too dark and even that is destroyed) and much higher bitterness than lighter roasted coffees.

5 First crack before development

6 First crack after development

7 Continuing development and darkening

8 Second crack

9 French roast (very dark)

COOLING

We're judging the coffee right up until the point where we open the door of the drum and drop the hot coffee beans into the cooling tray. The intense heat of the beans extends the roasting even when it hits the tray, which has air drawn through by a powerful fan. Correctly anticipating the end point of the roast requires precision timing to release the batch at just the right moment, knowing it will run on for a short time. And this is modified by the seasons and room temperature. We aim to air-cool the coffee within 3 minutes: this helps retain sweetness.

Some roasters use a quenching system, which sprays water onto the coffee, evaporating off as steam and removing heat. This can help arrest the roast, but from our experience it compromises the retention of freshness.

The roast profile

When looking at the progression of a roast, time and temperature are our markers. On our roasters we have a temperature probe that sits at a point where the beans are pooling as they tumble in the roasting drum, and here we read off the coffee bean temperature.

The graph starts after preheating to the charge temperature, when the green beans are dropped into the roasting drum. The temperature drops, then climbs as the beans begin to absorb heat. Our roasters watch the rate of change of temperature, and at the key points they gently adjust the flame to keep things moving along at just the right pace.

EXAMPLE OF A ROAST PROFILE

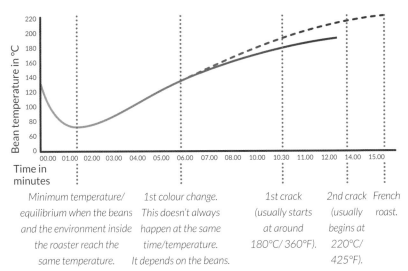

Bean temperature in °C

220 200 180 160 140 120 100 80 60 0

00.00 01.00 02.00 03.00 04.00 05.00 06.00 07.00 08.00 10.00 10.30 11.00 12.00 14.00 15.00

Time in minutes

Minimum temperature/ equilibrium when the beans and the environment inside the roaster reach the same temperature.

1st colour change. This doesn't always happen at the same time/temperature. It depends on the beans.

1st crack (usually starts at around 180°C/ 360°F).

2nd crack (usually begins at 220°C/ 425°F).

French roast.

The chart shows two different possible roasts and results for a given coffee. The solid line represents a 'medium' roast finishing between 1st and 2nd crack. The dotted line after first colour change follows a higher temperature and will run on to 2nd crack or French roast if desired.

FIRES

You've either just had one or you just haven't had one yet! All roasters experience fires, even with regular cleaning, especially if they produce many dark roasts. When you are well into your roasting run, an ember from a bean near second crack lifts into the airflow, and may make it through the exhaust duct and into the chaff collector. Then it drops into the chaff bucket below, igniting huge volumes of the chaff. The paint begins to peel and the pipes glow red like a Harley after a 100-mile blast down the freeway: that's a chaff fire. The other type of fire is way scarier. Once or twice we've had a power failure during the roast and when that happens the drum stops turning, the fans shut down and the beans can combust inside the drum. This is what we refer to as A Real Disaster: if the fire continues, the entire drum (the most expensive part of your roaster) can warp and distort in the heat.

A battery of 'pull-out roasters' in action in Boston, USA, mid-19th century. The roasting drums were heated by large furnaces and when fully operational it must have seemed like the fires of hell. Today the flames are more controlled, but fires do occasionally happen.

HOME ROASTING

Some people swear by their stovetop coffee roaster, insisting that they get great coffee from those hand-roasted beans – and a lot of satisfaction from the process itself. (As people who find coffee roasting to be a truly captivating activity, we can certainly relate to that second part.) If you're determined to go the home-roasted route, we're not going to argue with you. Several electric home roasting machines are available nowadays but these can vary greatly in cost. These machines will give repeatable (and drinkable) results more quickly and easily than the stovetop or oven methods. We have chosen to show the popcorn-popper pan method here as it's the first way of roasting we ever tried – and it's cheap to buy!

JUST REMEMBER A FEW THINGS:

• Roasting takes a long time to master, and you're likely to get some less-than-wonderful results when you're learning.

• Roasting beans produce a lot of smoke. Be prepared – and make sure your extractor is switched on to High. Open a window, too.

• Stand by the machine the whole time, not just so you can crank the handle but so you can follow the roast with your eyes and ears.

• Have a metal colander at the ready so you can tip the beans into it as soon as they come out of the roaster.

1 Measure 225–250g (8–9oz) of green coffee beans and put them into a small, clean, dry cup or jug. Heat the roaster over a medium heat until it is very hot. If you have a stand-alone oven thermometer, put it in the roaster and wait until it reads 200°C (400°F). Take the thermometer out, put in the beans and close the lid. Start cranking the handle immediately and continue regularly throughout. Keep constant watch on the beans and adjust the temperature as needed: don't let them start to smoke too early, but if they're taking too long, turn the heat up a little.

2 After around 6 minutes, you will start to see smoke and the first crack will begin (you'll hear popping noises). This is when you need to take maximum care. Don't be afraid to take the roaster off the heat if you think things are going too fast, and turn down the heat just a little if you want to. About a minute after first crack begins, check the beans often – every 30 seconds is best, or at least every minute. As soon as the beans take on the desired colour for a light-to-medium roast, they are ready: this might take anything from 8–10 minutes. Tip them into the colander and shake it gently but firmly so the beans get as much air as possible: they need to cool down quickly to stop the roast.

Note: stop roasting just before the coffee reaches its final colour; the beans retain heat and will continue to roast until their temperature drops. Some people use a desk fan over the colander to promote rapid cooling.

3 If you want a darker roast, continue roasting for another 1–2 minutes. Take great care at this stage, as beans can pass from dark-roast to scorched very quickly. Tip the beans into the colander and shake it gently but firmly so the beans get as much air as possible.

CHOOSING COFFEE

Over the years since we started Union, we've wanted to give our customers as much information and therefore confidence as possible. We wanted people to know that what we are trying to do is real and honest and not a marketing confection. Transparency has always been our watchword and from day one we talked about the country and region of origin, the coffee variety, and how it was harvested and proce ced. These are useful reference points that certainly helped us in our own learning as we tasted our way around the world. Coffee shares this element of terroir with the wine world – unsurprisingly so. When labels provide navigable information, then our experience can build the ability to make choices.

Roaster

The first choice is who to buy from. There are increasing numbers of small and large roasting companies on the internet, most of whom can send coffee by mail order for a nominal cost. Each roaster may have their own ethos around the quality (cost) of coffees that they buy and their approach to roasting and taste. I'd liken this to choosing craft beers, and many coffee explorers are taking this approach – finding a roaster whose 'house style' they like. At Union we often talk about letting the coffees speak for themselves, allowing their character to shine: we try to find the natural signature of each coffee and roast according to its needs. For us, this is generally a lighter roast. If you prefer a darker roast, another roaster may well be the one for you.

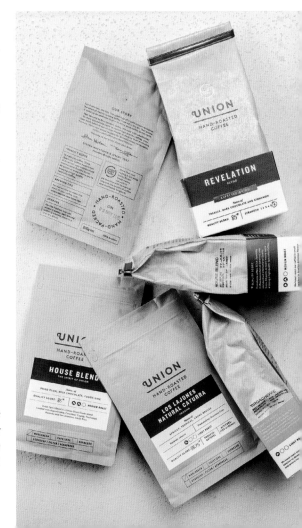

Blend or single origin

After the company's name, the second most prominent descriptor on the pack will probably be the one that indicates whether the coffee is a blend – composed of coffees from more than one country – or a single origin, where all of the coffee comes from one country.

Our mail order and grocery store coffee bags. Both offer the same quality coffee but our bags to be sold in other stores have a bit more colour to make them easily discernible. Mail order users often seek more detailed information (along with roaster-direct freshness) such as process method and varietal.

UNDERSTANDING BLENDS

For many coffee drinkers, the constituents of a blend are less important than the overall flavour profile or character, which has to be consistent throughout the year and from one year to the next. Blends can offer greatness, but for many companies they also provide the cloak of security and financial opportunity.

Our view of blending at Union is centred on our work with espresso brewing. (I hesitate to say 'espresso coffee' as in reality there is no such thing! Espresso is a brewing method, not a type of coffee, and its resulting short black drink is a very particular expression of the coffee beans.) The process intensifies certain characteristics and radically changes many elements of the in-cup balance when compared to the same coffee made in a filter or cafetière method. It's almost like playing a CD and turning the treble up and the bass down: that rich sound mix can be lost, so we need to optimize the coffees for this brewing method – creating a cup that has a beginning, a middle and an end. When a well-crafted blend is correctly prepared it can offer all the great experiences of coffee, and it should be the same day in, day out. Arguably, this is what most coffee companies and café bars are built upon: familiarity and comfort.

Sometimes, however, blending is done to arrive at a lower or managed cost; we call this the 'burgerization' of coffee. We all know burger chains that will give you a 'safe dose' of protein anywhere around the world. Managing flavour to a point where no single aspect dominates makes a bland but highly repeatable and cost-effective product. These recipes allow companies, whether sourcing beef, lager or coffee, to roam around the world seeking out low-cost producers whose products do not shift the taste. It's OK, and it's sometimes useful; but you wouldn't ask them to cook you a 28-day dry-aged ribeye steak.

READING THE BLENDED LABEL

Labels on blends are generally of two types. In one, the coffee is named after a 'primary' country of origin, for example 'Kenya Blend', which should suggest that the coffee has a character broadly reminiscent of the country's average style. There's no indication of regionality (like a vin de France, as opposed to an identifiable Burgundy or Bordeaux). There is no way of judging the quality of the blend except by trying it. With luck, it will be composed of good coffees only from that country. But it might be a percentage of decent Kenya beans, which are often sold at a quality premium, filled out with a larger percentage of neutral 'filler' coffees – coffees that have no discernible character and which can be bought cheaply, from anywhere in the world – to manage cost to the roaster.

The other approach is to give names that are either indicative of a 'serving suggestion', such as Breakfast Blend or After Dinner Blend, or more 'spiritual' ones that appeal to the style or culture of the roaster and their brand. We have recently seen a coffee labelled 'Rainforest Blend', which sounds very evocative but which gives no sense of how it will taste.

Are any of these names particularly useful to the coffee explorer? Unless clear taste notes are presented on the pack or in online descriptions, we would suggest that these styles are best chosen once you have a feel for the various markers of quality and can discern the differences. At the most basic level, checking to see if blends are 100 per cent Arabica or contain some Robusta coffee will give a guide as to how 'clean' the tastes may be. Robusta will always add some muddiness of flavour, albeit with an increased body and some dark sugar notes. Unfortunately for the explorer, we also need to remember that many levels of quality exist even in the world of Arabica, some being no better than the average Robusta. Tasting, trial and experience always have to be our guides.

Single-origin coffees

As the name implies, these come from just one country – or sometimes from a single district or farm. Just as provenance and traceability are becoming more desirable in a wide range of foods and drinks, roasters are increasingly offering coffees that are the product of a single farm or district. This is getting us even closer to true expression of terroir and the recognition that even within a single country or region, some areas are more blessed by nature and some farmers are more capable of achieving maximum quality in their beans.

On the basis that the fewer the ingredients, the harder they have to work, coffees from one district or producer, referred to as single estate, are usually selected because they have higher intrinsic cup quality and offer a clear expression of their region. As you continue your coffee exploration, these are the beans that should claim an increasing part of your attention.

Caution should be taken with single-origin designation by a roaster known for budget coffees if something unusually promising is on offer – this is where knowing the reputation of the roaster can help you arrive at a trustworthy selection. If they usually deal in costume jewellery, do they have the skills to find and appreciate a diamond?

MICRO-LOTS

Let's say you have an apple orchard. Most of the trees produce great apples, but in one area the apples are amazingly great: crisper and juicier than the rest of the orchard. Generally, all of the fruit from the entire orchard is mixed and sold together. But what if you pick out the best apples to sell them separately?

That's the idea of micro-lot. Micro-lot coffee is almost always quality coffee (although of course not all quality coffee is micro-lot). The term refers to coffee that is kept separate from a farm's larger production. It is very difficult to produce consistent quality on an entire farm. One hectare on the north side may be a bit better than a plot on the east side of the land, and it's rare to know exactly why, since the next year the situation may reverse. Often, when a farmer finds a particular area that produces a better-tasting coffee than the rest of his land, that plot is harvested and processed separately.

When we say a coffee is micro-lot, we are then referring to the fact that the farmer puts extra effort into harvesting it and then not mixing it with the rest of the farm's output. This approach takes time and money, and we pay significant premiums for such coffee. Most of the time, we at Union would pay around twice the Fairtrade price. For an exceptional micro-lot, we pay a substantial premium over those prices in order to give the farmer the incentive to make the extra effort.

These exceptional micro-lots may represent anything from just one or two 60–69kg sacks up to around 20 or 30 sacks. Given these small volumes, it is rare to find micro-lots in any chain or larger supermarket; they are usually found at roasters' own outlets or online and can be fleeting in their availability. Once you have developed your taste for a wider range of coffee styles, this approach to your coffee drinking can be hugely rewarding.

A MEMORABLE MICRO-LOT

Although our micro-lot collection at Union is a small part of our yearly buying, it offers the chance to stumble upon something really amazing. On one of Jeremy's trips to Costa Rica, having tasted several tables of samples (each with as many as 30 or 40 cups), the last table of five or six sample lots had to be fitted in before leaving for the flight home. 'On that very table was a single cup that delighted me, reminding me of a clean, elegant Sauvignon Blanc wine: fruity but with a mineral structure that held on the palate and with notes of white peach, vanilla and cane sugar. Running out the door, I jumped into the car and on the way to the airport phoned the office, got the name of the producer and agreed a price for a two-sack lot, just 130kg of green coffee among several tonnes I had marked for purchase that week. I did make the flight, only just. And we are still buying that coffee five years later.'

DOES ORGANIC COFFEE TASTE BETTER?

There are good-tasting organic coffees and there are bad ones. The flavour profile of coffee, its sweetness, acidity, bitterness and mouth feel, is unrelated to any certification. Organic, Fairtrade and other such words on the label do not guarantee a good cup. High-quality coffee stems from good soils, climate, altitude and dedicated farmers who put a tremendous effort into harvesting and processing their cherries. Within the organic rules and regulations there are some practices that most likely will have a positive effect on flavour profile, such as the use of organic compost, taking preventive soil erosion measures and shade-grown coffee. If managed correctly on the farm, these will lead to increased soil quality, which will probably have a positive effect on taste.

BUYING IN A SHOP

More and more of us are buying our beans by mail order nowadays, once we've discovered a roaster whose coffees we like. Sometimes you may need to buy from a shop: if you do, you'll be lucky to find beans from your own preferred roaster. So, in the spirit of exploration, look for the name of a roaster you have heard good things about. In general, whoever the roaster is, you should look on the label of pre-packed beans for a roasting date. If the label doesn't say, ask the staff at the shop. Provided that the coffee has been packed carefully (which it will be in most shops and supermarkets) and oxygen excluded from the pack, the coffee will be fine for three or four weeks after roasting. Buy whole beans rather than ground coffee, and if they ask whether you would like it ground, give them a polite no thanks.

STORING YOUR COFFEE

Fresh air is the mortal enemy of coffee. Why? Because fresh coffee is hygroscopic: it absorbs moisture – and everything else in its environment, including oxygen and odours. The fridge is one of the worst places to store fresh coffee. Fridges ooze with distinct, pungent aromas. Your coffee soaks them up like a sponge. Do you want your rich, intense espresso to take on hints of three-day-old onion or Cheddar cheese? Didn't think so.

Once opened, a bag of whole-bean coffee starts losing its flavour after one week. Ground coffee? After an hour. So store your coffee in a dry, stable environment, and brew it within 14 days of purchase. You can store it in the freezer, in an airtight container, but take out only what you need for the day's brew and then reseal. Do this quickly to avoid repeated condensation on the beans, which will detract from flavour in the cup.

BREWING

Brewing is the final stop in the coffee bean's long journey from the farm where it was grown to the cup in front of the consumer. In a café or restaurant, a professional will be completing that journey. At home, it's up to you. Whichever method you choose, none is better or 'more authentic' than the others – the important thing is that you like the taste of your coffee.

Behind the apparent simplicity of the equation coffee + water = pleasurable drink, there are many variables. Learning a little about why coffee tastes the way it does, and how to recognize and describe flavours and aromas, will help you decide which coffee to buy and how to brew it. From weighing to grinding to extracting, every stage of brewing shapes the final cup in different ways. Exploring those variables will help you find out what you really like, and how to make your perfect cup of coffee.

THE CHEMISTRY OF COFFEE

Well over 800 flavour and aroma compounds have been discovered in brewed coffee, and one of the most exciting aspects of coffee for us is understanding how and why they arise. Several books cover coffee chemistry, but for the non-chemist, reading them can be very much the antidote to caffeine! So we will look only at the main cast members.

The two main classes of compounds we are interested in (as coffee roasters and drinkers) are carbohydrates (sugars) and organic acids. To understand the interplay between these two groups, think of the difference between a cheap white wine and a 'decent' bottle. The cheap wine may be sharp, with a thin, short feel on the palate due to a lack of supporting sweetness and the dominance of just one or two acids. Better wine has a pleasing balance of crisp, clean flavours coming from a mix of a wider range of acids, some of which also impart a sense of sweetness or fruitiness over which all the flavours and aromas are layered.

Acids

A number of broadly familiar acids such as citric acid (found in oranges, lemons and limes) and malic acid occur naturally within the unroasted coffee bean; others, like acetic acid, arise from the breakdown or interaction of particular sugars and other compounds. The precise proportions of each acid and hence the perceived quality or complexity of the coffee depend on a wide range of factors such as the variety of coffee tree, minerals in the soil, temperature and humidity, as well as on the degree of roast. The largest acid component present in unroasted coffee is a family of chlorogenic acids (CGAs), which account for around 5–10 per cent of the dry weight of unroasted coffee beans. They are characterized by grassy, bright or sour flavours and also contribute bitterness to coffee. A significant proportion of these break down in roasting to yield other acids, such as caffeic and quinic acids, that are less overtly bitter or sour and which at lower concentrations in the final brew contribute to the complex bitter-sweet nature of coffee.

CGAs have also come to interest health-conscious consumers because they are part of a family of compounds called polyphenols, which have been recognized for their antioxidant properties and have been found by some studies to lower risk of heart disease and some cancers.

Sugars

One of the most important sugars present in coffee is sucrose; it can contribute significant sweetness to the final brew. During roasting it breaks down as the roast progresses to darker shades; this is one reason why darker roasted coffee tastes less sweet and more bitter than light roasts. This change happens as sugar molecules caramelize and undergo a reaction with proteins known as the Maillard reaction, which is responsible for the brown colour of coffee as well as a huge array of aromatic compounds. Throughout the roast, at various stages, both caramelization and the Maillard reaction are under way, the former being responsible for aromas like sweet caramel, butterscotch and vanilla, the latter contributing the 'roasty' notes as well as floral, savoury or chocolate tones.

Sucrose development in the coffee cherry peaks with ripening. That is one reason why at Union we spend so much time visiting producers around harvest to ensure that pickers work selectively and pick only fully ripe coffee cherries. Robusta coffee contains notably less sucrose (as well as lower levels of CGAs) than Arabica and this is why Robusta coffee is less complex in flavours developed in roasting as well as being more bitter than Arabica.

Other compounds

Another significant group of compounds in the coffee bean is alkaloids. This group contains the most famous component of coffee, caffeine, as well as a lesser-known compound called trigonelline. Caffeine is the stimulant that first brought coffee beans to human attention and for many it remains the functional reason to drink and crave coffee. It has a bitter flavour, and this bitterness is part of the overall flavour profile of coffee. Trigonelline is similarly bitter-tasting, although it is degraded by roasting, and also contributes to the formation of a large number of highly aromatic compounds. During roasting trigonelline is largely broken down into niacin, or vitamin B3, accounting for up to 1–3mg per cup (depending upon strength and brewing style, with more in espresso, less in filter), so two or three cups a day can contribute significantly to your recommended requirement of 14–18mg a day.

WATER MATTERS

Water is the hidden ingredient in coffee: it makes up around 90–98 per cent of the cup's contents. If you are one of the many people who feel there's a taste difference between tap water and bottled spring water, remember that that difference will also appear in your brewed coffee.

Though completely safe to drink, tap water often has a slight or pronounced chlorine taste from treatment of the water. Hard water will also have a dry, clear mineral-like quality from a higher-than-average presence of certain calcium and magnesium ions, while softer water (with a lower mineral load) may yield a sweeter taste. Another important component is bicarbonates, salts that balance the acidity/alkalinity of the water. Though broadly neutral in taste, they make a considerable difference to the flavours perceived in the final brew. For optimum coffee brewing, water should be close to neutral (pH 7), neither acid nor alkaline.

The minerals with the biggest effect on our perception of taste are calcium and magnesium, which we can see in the white deposits from scale formation in our kettles, coffee machines and all household appliances that heat water. Most bottled waters are sold with mineral and other components within a much narrower range than domestic sources, and unless you live in an area that is blessed with soft water, you may find bottled water cleaner to the taste. Different sources also yield different amounts of insoluble particles. Though mostly filtered out from the domestic supply, they can leave a slight turbidity or chalkiness.

It should not be surprising that if an 'off taste' is found in the water then it will also be present behind the taste of the coffee. While many home users making tea or coffee regularly with the same brand will have adapted to it, when tasting something new, it can get in the way of experiencing what the tea blender or coffee roaster presents in tasting notes on the pack. When you begin exploring different roasts, origins and blends, a little experimentation with water can yield amazing results.

Most coffee roasters, when tasting their coffees, will use specially designed filter systems to remove any flavour taint such as chlorine, as well as turbidity to leave the water crystal clear. In addition, special resins are used to remove most of the calcium and magnesium ions, or to bind them with non-reactive sodium to prevent the formation of scale inside expensive espresso and filter machines.

If you live in an area with soft to moderately hard water, a carbon filter may be all you need to get a clean, well-brewed cup of coffee. Simple jug filters and cartridge-based under-sink systems fitted to the kitchen tap will give immediately noticeable results when compared to using tap water. Some filter manufacturers suggest making tea with filtered versus unfiltered water and observing the difference – the tea brewed with filtered water appears clearer and without the 'scum' or film that appears at the surface or around the rim of the cup.

In choosing a more active filter system, however, it's not a case of less is more. Taking out all the minerals can devastate the flavour and aroma of the coffee. Typical (domestic) water softeners may strip out too much of the mineral content and they should be adapted to allow a small percentage of non-filtered water to bypass the filter. As an experiment, try brewing your regular coffee with de-ionized water (with all the minerals stripped out) from a pharmacy: the coffee tastes flat and dull. We need some minerals as they are part of the chemistry of extracting flavour from the coffee

grounds. So calcium and magnesium need to be present in roughly the 'right amount': too high or too low in concentration and the brew may be flat and closed to flavour and aroma.

For these reasons, coffee lovers living in hard water areas may be best served by experimenting with bottled spring water as an alternative to filter systems. Bear in mind the wide range of minerality levels between brands and sources. Research by coffee standards organizations around the world has resulted in a broad consensus as to the optimum balance of minerals (see table below). This may be useful in comparing the bottled waters available in your area.

TYPES OF FILTER

Whichever type of filter you use, remember that its lifespan will be determined by the purity of the incoming water. Higher mineral levels or more turbidity will reduce the overall volume of water that the filter can handle. Most filter manufacturers recommend replacement at least every six months.

Active charcoal/carbon

A basic cartridge, fitted in a jug filter or under the sink. These only remove off-tastes or cloudiness. No effect upon hardness.

Ion exchange

Often referred to as anti-scale cartridges, these usually incorporate an active carbon filter as well as a resin that 'grabs' the calcium and magnesium and 'swaps' them for low levels of sodium.

Reverse osmosis (RO)

Increasingly found in high-end cafés where a high level of purity is required, this process uses a special membrane under pressure to remove all impurities. These filters have a significantly higher running cost than cartridge-based methods. As total mineral removal is not suitable for coffee or tea brewing, RO systems developed for coffee machines and catering use may have an adjustable bypass where a small percentage of unfiltered water is injected back into the filtered output to give a precise mineral content.

GOOD WATER GUIDELINES

The Specialty Coffee Association of America suggests the following guidelines for the perfect water to brew your coffee. Look online for a water testing kit to test your domestic water (with or without filtration), or look at the label on bottled water for much of this information. Chlorides may be listed on the label – these are not the same as chlorine and are not harmful; chloride levels in unpolluted water are around 10mg/litre and to affect the taste the level would need to be more than 200mg/litre.

Characteristic	Target
Odour	Clean, fresh, odour-free
Colour	Clear
Total chlorine	0mg/litre
Total dissolved solids at 180°C (360°F) – on bottled water this is described as 'dry residue at 180°C'	150mg/litre
Calcium hardness	4 grains or 68mg/litre
Total alkalinity	40mg/litre
pH	7
Sodium	10mg/litre

EXPLORING COFFEE'S FLAVOURS

Our experience of coffee is influenced by a range of personal as well as physiological factors. When talking to coffee drinkers, whether they have one cup a day or are serious serial-brew junkies spending most of the day grinding, pouring and drinking, most of them talk about how strong, mild, smooth or bitter the cup is. These terms mostly address the physical aspect of the coffee, how it sits on the palate, rather than the more alluring aromatic characteristics. The total sum of all sensory responses to a coffee, or indeed to any food or drink, is referred to as its organoleptic quality.

To see this in action, think about eating when you have a heavy head cold. A slice of orange or lemon will be virtually indistinguishable from one another. Both may feel sharp on the tongue, but without the lemon or orange aroma both are merely experienced as citric by the acid receptors on the tongue. Perceptions of what coffee is and how it should taste are often limited by our previous experience. Many view it as a 'functional food' to wake them up, so it needs to be strong and dark and bitter. Others seek a mild, smooth or milky cup that may be more about marking a moment in the day – perhaps with a slice of cake. In our world of discovering and roasting coffees, such simple views are a thing of the past. We know how better farming practices continue to improve coffee crops, and farmers and roasters increasingly talk about what consumers want and how they can produce it. There has been an explosion of interest in coffee: look into many specialist independent cafés and you'll find alluring descriptions of fruits, nuts and chocolate references as respectful brewing meets enthusiastic consumers.

To help understand what flavours and aromas are present in coffee, the Speciality Coffee Association of America (SCAA) in 1995 came up with a useful tool called the Flavour Wheel. This diagrammatic representation was developed from a similar tool in the wine industry and grouped families of flavours together along with their process or roasting causative factors and helps to inform trainees in coffee as to what and how certain characteristics developed. For the average coffee drinker it's a little hard to read, so recently our friends at Counter Culture Coffee based in Durham, North Carolina, USA, developed what we think is a much more user-friendly version, pictured on the facing page.

On the inner circle the wheel groups families of flavours which expand on the outer layer into more specific flavours, all of which with experience can be variously found in high-quality coffees. The two boxes to the left show descriptors for the physical feel of the body and those we commonly use to describe the characteristic of a coffee's acidity. Both of these boxes can be used in conjunction with the more specific taste descriptors to build your sense of the coffee and to clearly communicate it to others sharing the experience.

The most difficult aspect of using the wheel is that of being honest with ourselves as to which flavours we are genuinely detecting and not

TEST YOUR TASTE RECEPTORS

To demonstrate the physical aspects of taste, make up a very dilute solution of salt, sugar, lemon juice and, if you have them, a drop or two of bitters as used in cocktails. At very dilute levels you will find that different areas of the tongue respond, but any sense of 'flavour' conferred by aromatics is not present.

suggesting those which we don't taste or think we do. Even though it may look daunting, it can be a great tool to start developing a language of taste and flavour and is a handy prompt to keep with you when starting your cupping and tasting adventures. A great and enjoyable way to quickly build your skills is to taste with a friend, keep quiet and make your own notes first then compare notes to see how similar an experience you've had.

Many of the commonly found flavours in coffee can be described as:

Floral Jasmine, blossom-like
Fruity Citrus, apple-like, red berries
Nutty Praline/hazelnut, almond
Chocolate Milk chocolate, dark chocolate, cocoa

L I G H T	WATERY	
	TEA-LIKE	
	SILKY	
	SLICK	
	JUICY	
M E D I U M	SMOOTH	
	2% MILK	
	SYRUPY	
	ROUND	
	CREAMY	
H E A V Y	FULL	
	VELVETY	
	BIG	
	CHEWY	
	COATING	

INTENSIFIERS FOR COFFEE

CRISP BRIGHT VIBRANT TART	MUTED DULL MILD
WILD UNBALANCED SHARP POINTED	STRUCTURED BALANCED ROUNDED
DENSE DEEP COMPLEX	SOFT FAINT DELICATE
JUICY	DRY ASTRINGENT
LINGERING DIRTY	QUICK CLEAN

FLAVOUR WHEEL

© Counter Culture Coffee

SEEKING QUALITY IN THE CUP

What is quality in a coffee? How can we say one coffee from Guatemala may or may not be better than one from Ethiopia when they present such different cups? Is my preference for one style over another an expression of quality? No! It's the same as in judging wine: how do you compare the quality of a Chablis with a Chianti? The answer lies in learning to separate objective and subjective opinion, and 'cupping' gives us this tool.

A coffee buyer, whatever the company they work for, has a series of decisions to make: how good is a particular coffee, is it worth the money being asked by the producer and – importantly, recognizing that many levels of quality and therefore price exist – is it the sort of coffee that meets the commercial need of the company? In most cases of commercial (commodity) coffee, it's mainly a matter of screening out batches with natural defects (e.g. immature beans) or flaws that arise from mechanical handling or post-harvest processing, leading to undesirable flavours.

'Cupping' is different. Also referred to as 'liquoring' in the export houses of Kenya, this is a protocol that allows buyers and roasters to taste and compare many samples from different farms, regions or even countries and to evaluate them in a strictly objective manner. All of the samples are prepared in exactly the same way so that any difference between cups can only be due to the nature of the bean and not the brewing. The most direct way to brew samples for tasting is simply to pour water over grounds, allow it time to steep and then get in there and sniff, slurp and taste.

STANDARDIZING THE ROAST

If we are investigating parcels of green coffee, we first need to standardize the degree of roast. As coffees are roasted progressively darker, the many elements of flavour change (see chapter 2), and to evaluate these fairly we use a small 'sample roaster' that allows us to roast about 100g (4oz) of beans. Each sample is roasted to a light roast.

We often liken the process of cupping to contact sheets from the old days of photography: negatives are laid on photographic paper and all exposed identically. This allows the photo editor to compare images before selecting the best one and printing it carefully to bring out the best in it. In our coffee world, the sample roast is our contact sheet. From it we decide how we roast them for brewing so that all of the flavours in them are evident and well balanced.

A busy day in our cupping lab. We're tasting daily production batches, so only three cups per sample. If it's a new coffee we're evaluating, it can be up to six per sample.

Cupping the professional way

When we set up our cuppings at Union, we prepare multiple cups of each coffee so that we can ensure that the coffee is consistent. This reduces the chance that a lot will be spoiled by rogue beans (which indicates an overall lack of care and attention in producing the beans). If a coffee is new to us, we prepare a minimum of six cups at each stage; if it's a coffee that we want to refresh our opinion of, three or four cups will be made.

In our lab, we brew the coffees in small heatproof glasses with a capacity of around 200ml (7fl oz). First we weigh out 13g (½oz) of beans into each glass. This is then tipped into a grinder, set to a medium–fine grind. Every sample is ground separately and placed back in its glass so that any defective bean only affects the vessel that it sits in.

With all of the samples ground and placed upon the table, we first evaluate the aromas and fragrance of the ground coffee. We are interested in how exciting the aromas are – as we want you to be – and through experience we can pick up aspects that may indicate problems in how the coffee was produced.

After the 'dry' evaluation, all the glasses are filled with water, filtered and at between 92°C and 94°C (around 205°F), just about 30 seconds off the boil. With many cups on the table, all cups are poured as quickly and steadily as possible and a timer is started to give 4 minutes of steeping time. As the water is poured in, the grounds are wetted and rise to the top of the cup, forming a crust or cap in the glass, which holds in all of the wonderful (or otherwise) aromas.

After the steeping time, the fun really begins. Next is to evaluate the 'wet' or brewed aromas. For this we lean in very close over each cup and use a spoon to 'break the crusts' and all of the captured aromas rise. To encourage all of the aromas to come forward, we stir each cup three or four times: each cup is treated exactly the same, as stirring drives the coffee to brew deeper. We gently and repeatedly inhale, sniffing like a dog, to keep all the aromas in our noses and not take them deep into the lungs and chest (where we cannot detect their aromas). After adding the water, some of the aromas may be more subdued, others wildly pronounced; this is another opportunity for an experienced taster to identify good and bad aspects.

Specialty Coffee Association of America Cupping Form

Name: _____ Session: _____

Date: 08/09/15 Table: 3

Classification:

6.00 - Good	7.00 - Very Good	8.00 - Excellent	9.00 - Outstanding
6.25	7.25	8.25	9.25
6.50	7.50	8.50	9.50
6.75	7.75	8.75	9.75

Sample # JH #07
Red Icatu
Natural
16 bags

- Fragrance/Aroma Total: 8.5 Qualidad Dry/Crust
- Flavor Total: 8.25
- Aftertaste Total: 7.5
- Acidity Total: 8 Intensity High/Low
- Body Total: 8 Intensity High/Low
- Uniformity Total: 10
- Balance Total: 8.25
- Clean Cup: Total: 10
- Sweetness Total: 10
- Overall Total: 8.5
- Defects (subtract) Taint=2 Fault=4 # of cups ___ × Intensity ___ =
- **Total Score: 87**

Notes: Dry: Tropical fruit, pineapple, milk chocolate, vanilla //Wet: Ripe fruit. Sour intensity. Burst of flavor. Acidity round and smooth. A bit astringent as cools down. Custard.

Final Score: 87

Sample # Monte Alto NI
Red Bourbon
Natural
110 bags

- Fragrance/Aroma Total: 7 Quality Dry/Crust
- Flavor Total: 7.25
- Aftertaste Total: 8
- Acidity Total: 7.25 Intensity High/Low
- Body Total: 8.25 Intensity High/Low
- Uniformity Total: 8
- Balance Total: 7.5
- Clean Cup: Total: 8
- Sweetness Total: 10
- Overall Total: 7
- Defects (subtract) Taint=2 Fault=4 # of cups 1 × Intensity 4 = 4
- **Total Score: 78.25**

Notes: Dry: Banana, green notes. Roasted hazelnut //Cup: Hint of raspberry, lactic, fermentation in #3. Tropical fruits. Lingering coffee aftertaste. NOT APPROVED

Final Score: 74.25

Sample # Ellen #08
Yellow Catuai
Natural
53 bags

- Fragrance/Aroma Total: 8.25 Quality Dry/Crust
- Flavor Total: 7.75
- Aftertaste Total: 7.5
- Acidity Total: 8.5 Intensity High/Low
- Body Total: 7.5 Intensity High/Low
- Uniformity Total: 10
- Balance Total: 7.5
- Clean Cup: Total: 10
- Sweetness Total: 10
- Overall Total: 8
- Defects (subtract) Taint=2 Fault=4 # of cups ___ × Intensity ___ =
- **Total Score: 85.25**

Notes: Peach. Coffee blossom. Tea Rose. //Candy-like sweetness but less complex than expected./Thins out. Citric acidity. Jammy. Slightly dry cocoa aftertaste.

Final Score: 85.25

Sample #
Roast level ___

- Fragrance/Aroma Total: ___
- Flavor Total: ___
- Aftertaste Total: ___
- Acidity Total: ___
- Body Total: ___
- Uniformity Total: ___
- Balance Total: ___
- Clean Cup: Total: ___
- Sweetness Total: ___
- Overall Total: ___
- Defects (subtract) Taint=2 Fault=4 # of cups ___ × Intensity ___ =
- **Total Score: ___**

Notes:

Final Score: ___

Facing page: The cupping form breaks down our experience of the sample into different categories and allows us to apply an overall quality score to the coffee. It is here that experience really counts. An experienced taster will be able to give a score for each category that represents how close that coffee comes to our ideal, a view that is inevitably based upon all of the cups we have ever tasted, but which should be attainable, if nature has truly shone upon the farm with just the right amount of rain, sun, soil quality and harvesting care.

Below: Scoring and giving a cupper's view of a coffee's quality means nothing unless all cuppers, especially those of producers and their buyers, agree the meaning of their scores and have clear expectations of what to expect from a sample. In order to standardize and create an international language, the Specialty Coffee Association of America (SCAA) has implemented a scoring system that has been adopted globally by those participating in the value-added speciality coffee trade.

The cups then need time to cool to a point at which our taste buds can cope with the diversity of flavours and characteristics. For anyone who routinely drinks their coffee (or tea) scalding hot, please take note – taste buds are less sensitive at higher temperatures (above around 65°C/150°F). During this time, we scoop from the surface any grounds that continue to float so that when we actually taste, we are not distracted by 'bits'.

The tasting of coffee is then very similar to that of wine: we need to allow air to the sample so that the complex of flavours and aromas can be picked up by taste buds on the tongue and by the olfactory sensors in the nose. When we taste, we use a small bowl-shaped spoon and slurp loudly so as to spray the coffee over the palate. Just like wine tasters do, we hold the liquid in the mouth, head slightly forward so that the coffee stays near to the lips, and draw air through, then roll the coffee around the mouth. Over a few sips, we get a sense of the physical (how clean, smooth, silky, tart, light-, medium- or full-bodied is the coffee?) before even thinking about what it actually tastes like. Gradually, as the coffee cools and we take more sips, we can build up a picture of what we find, using a scoring form to guide us.

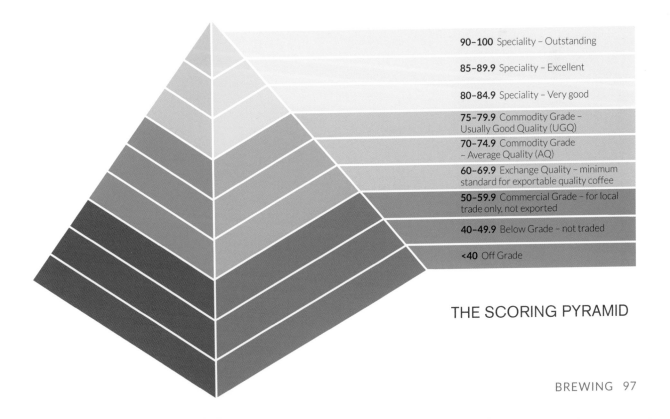

90–100 Speciality – Outstanding

85–89.9 Speciality – Excellent

80–84.9 Speciality – Very good

75–79.9 Commodity Grade – Usually Good Quality (UGQ)

70–74.9 Commodity Grade – Average Quality (AQ)

60–69.9 Exchange Quality – minimum standard for exportable quality coffee

50–59.9 Commercial Grade – for local trade only, not exported

40–49.9 Below Grade – not traded

<40 Off Grade

THE SCORING PYRAMID

The cupping form and the protocols described on the previous pages are simply 'the mechanics of cupping'. Giving meaningful scores depends upon a reasonable level of experience in tasting and assessing a wide range of quality coffees, developing in the cupper the ability to differentiate not only a speciality quality from low quality, but to be able to split out very small variations at the higher levels. This is important, as just one or two points can make the difference of several cents per pound (in weight) to the producer.

Grades scoring less than 60 points are not considered export quality and do not make it into even the low-cost international Arabica blends. To be accepted onto the New York exchange a sample must score at least 60 points. Coffees traded at between 60 and 70 points will have no regional character and may not offer much more than a 'coffee-flavoured' brew, and will usually lack sweetness and smoothness in the cup. Average and Usually Good Quality should also not be assumed to offer much for the speciality coffee drinker: these are still firmly in the commodity coffee end of the market, the province of vending, low-quality hotel or diner coffee.

The world of speciality coffees, those that offer some differentiation of flavour by region and that present a clean character, free of defects, start at the 80-point level. These coffees represent only around 5 per cent of world coffee production; those scoring 84 or more come from a pool of only around 3 per cent.

For a coffee to be regarded as excellent (85+) it has to present a range of clearly defined aromas and flavours. There should be a well developed acidity that combines the characteristics of citric, malic and other fruit acids – what we would recognize as 'juicy' if applied to fruits. It is worth saying that these truly great coffees do not always have to have wild, outlandish or BIG flavours; some of the best coffees we have come across are those that are like a well-made suit, wonderfully balanced without being showy! An amazing Colombia or Rwanda coffee can be every bit as good as a (currently) fashionable, flashy, honey Geisha coffee that can sell for significant premiums based upon its rarity.

It's here in our cupping lab that our inner coffee geek really comes out. Aside from standing next to our roasting machine as the beans tumble out into the cooling tray, the cupping lab is our favourite part of Union's roastery.

Steven, Jeremy and quality manager Rudy assessing various roast options for a new coffee. We score in detail and discuss so as to ensure the best presentation of a coffee's characteristics.

It's where all of our coffees begin their relationship with us and where even after 20 years of sourcing you can still find us skipping around the table with excitement when a truly wonderful coffee shows its colours.

The level of activity in our cupping lab is partly dependent on the time of year, but it is always a busy space. Every batch we roast – daily, during the various harvest seasons of Central America, East Africa and Indonesia – has to be evaluated. On any given day it's not uncommon for us to work through 20 or 30 samples, and with six cups of each, that's a heck of a lot of coffee to taste. Do we get wired with caffeine? Even though we spit most samples, the body does absorb some caffeine from each and a heavy day can leave us with screaming gums and a queasy buzz! A professional hazard, but a happy one, our equivalent of the post-gym muscle ache!

HOW TO TASTE COFFEE – CUPPING AT HOME

The cupping exercise is a great way for anyone seeking to understand more about coffee. For most people, comparing one coffee with another can be tricky. Laying out a few coffees to taste side by side can reveal some surprising detail. Over time, as we become more familiar with the major differences and begin to tune in to finer points of appreciation, our choices between one country of origin and another can hone in to a recognition of differences between regions and between the processing methods used to prepare the coffee after harvesting. By building up a sense of the variables, we are then able to search out the coffees we personally prefer.

Getting started

To begin cupping coffee at home, it's important to have as much information as possible on the coffees you intend to work with. You'll need to know:

- Country of origin (don't pick blends to start with)
- Processing method (washed, pulped natural/honey process, natural/dry)
- Degree of roast

Few packaged supermarket coffees carry enough information on the packs, but many quality-oriented small roasters sell their coffees online, where more space can be given to descriptions of where and how the coffees are produced, the main flavour descriptors, and the type of roast. In general the less information given may mean less care or consideration in the selection of the coffees and a higher chance of mediocre coffees being offered.

DISCOVERY PACK

Cupping notes don't have to be complicated. Below is the tasting sheet for our Discovery Pack (available online). It comes with four coffee samples to 'blind taste' and discover each of the major flavour groups – and which you prefer in a coffee.

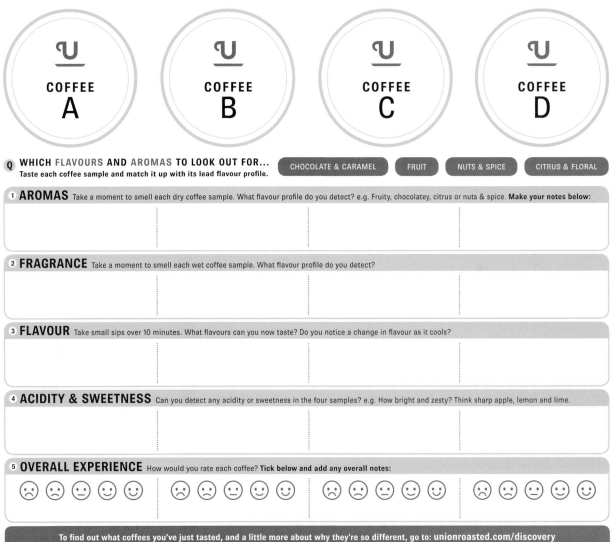

COFFEE A

COFFEE B

COFFEE C

COFFEE D

Q WHICH FLAVOURS AND AROMAS TO LOOK OUT FOR...
Taste each coffee sample and match it up with its lead flavour profile.

CHOCOLATE & CARAMEL   FRUIT   NUTS & SPICE   CITRUS & FLORAL

1 AROMAS Take a moment to smell each dry coffee sample. What flavour profile do you detect? e.g. Fruity, chocolatey, citrus or nuts & spice. **Make your notes below:**

2 FRAGRANCE Take a moment to smell each wet coffee sample. What flavour profile do you detect?

3 FLAVOUR Take small sips over 10 minutes. What flavours can you now taste? Do you notice a change in flavour as it cools?

4 ACIDITY & SWEETNESS Can you detect any acidity or sweetness in the four samples? e.g. How bright and zesty? Think sharp apple, lemon and lime.

5 OVERALL EXPERIENCE How would you rate each coffee? **Tick below and add any overall notes:**

To find out what coffees you've just tasted, and a little more about why they're so different, go to: **unionroasted.com/discovery**

We're not looking to be snobbish about this, but to learn what possibilities exist in a coffee style, it's best to avoid samples that may have defects, which will prevent the clearest expression of the coffee and will therefore confuse our learning.

A good selection of coffees to start with might be fully washed coffees from each of the major continental regions: Central America, South America, Africa and Indonesia, each of which present significantly different tastes. While the latter are predominantly naturally processed,

don't worry, as these coffees (notably from Sumatra and Java) are quite distinct from the other regions.

A modest investment in a dozen small heatproof glasses, a water filter jug and a decent home grinder will mean that you pretty much have your own cupping lab at hand and your journey can begin.

The drill

1 Weigh out 12–15g (about ½oz) beans into each glass – one glass of each coffee per person.

2 Grind each sample using the same setting on the grinder – aim for a medium–fine grind. After one coffee has been ground, to avoid mixing flavours in the grinder, eliminate any ground residues by flushing through with a small handful of the next bean chosen and discard that before grinding the tasting sample.

3 Boil fresh filtered or bottled water and allow to cool for 30 seconds before gently and steadily pouring over each sample to fill right up to the rim, ensuring that all of the grounds are wetted and no dry pockets remain.

4 Allow to steep for 4 minutes.

5 Using a soup spoon, break the crust that has formed, inhale the aromas and make a note of any characteristic that you can detect – any thought or opinion may be valid at this stage – stirring gently three or four times as you inhale. Get as close to each glass as you can without burning the tip of your nose! Try to stir each sample in roughly the same manner as you work across the glasses to ensure each brews similarly. Remember to pour an extra cup of hot water to rinse the spoon of grounds from one glass before digging into the next.

6 After the crust on each sample has been broken, most of the grounds will settle to the bottom; use the spoon to skim the surface, gently removing any remaining grounds that float.

7 Allow the samples to cool to a comfortable temperature.

8 Use the spoon to slurp the coffee so that it sprays across the palate and roll it around the mouth before spitting out or swallowing, and record any opinions you may have about the feel of the coffee in the mouth, its flavours and aromas.

Top: Cupping at home can be done with simple glasses and your own collected coffees; Bottom: To give people a chance to taste and test their skills, we developed a Discovery Pack with four samples and a self-guiding cupping form. Our samples A–D provide a range of flavour styles to detect your own preferences.

Learning how to taste

When recording your impressions, think first about the feel of the coffee. Is its acidity crisp like an apple, sharp and sour like a lemon? There are many foods that exhibit different styles of acidity, for example red fruits such as strawberry and redcurrant, and these can be valid when searching for descriptors for the acids, helping us to separate out the mildly tangy from mouthpuckering sourness. The sensation of acidity in the coffee along with its aromatics are what make up our total sense of the coffee flavour. Does it come across as sweet? If you usually drink coffee with sugar the cupping experience may seem challenging at first, but if the quality of coffee and roasting is good, then most tasters will soon be able to appreciate sweeter and less sweet coffee. Is there any bitterness or dryness in the finish? As you roll the coffee around your mouth, does it feel light or creamy-bodied?

Take repeated sips from the cup as you build your perception of the coffee, addressing each of these elements as you go and noting other food flavours that come to mind as you go through the samples. This part of tasting, 'tagging' the flavours and aromas, takes time to get comfortable with, but is what makes a good coffee taster. The most important thing is to be honest with yourself. Don't write down things you cannot really appreciate or recognize, and if you are tasting with another person, keep first thoughts to yourself to avoid being led to false conclusions. After each cup has been tasted and notes made, then by all means discuss what you find. This is where a common language will develop and your own appreciation and ability to recognize elements of a coffee will grow more quickly.

When we introduce people to this process, they often ask whether they should rinse the mouth with water or eat crackers to clean the palate between samples. Most professional coffee tasters tend not to do this as even plain foods can mask the palate and affect the physical feel of the coffee. Personally, we like to take a first pass along the samples on the table to 'season' our palates with some of the coffee oils present in the cups. We find that taking water between samples gets in the way of keeping the oils on the tongue and around the mouth. It's each to their own, however, and as long as you take a consistent approach it's your choice.

Further developments – and keeping it fun

To develop your ability to recall different characteristics, once you have done the cupping exercise with your first selected coffees, and (we hope) having found some differences between the samples, re-set the cupping with fresh samples and ask someone to come in and shuffle the samples around so that you do not know which is which. The goal then is to be able to recognize them from your tasting alone – this will be a test of how well and how honestly you record your impressions.

As your skills develop, seek out other coffee samples from your preferred roaster and choose perhaps different processing styles, or countries within one continent, or even regions within one country.

Remember, however, it's not a competition! It should be a fun exercise in finding out what you enjoy. Many people taking this route find after a while that they develop a wider preference – not just sticking with the one coffee they used to doggedly buy but a wider range that chimes with different circumstances – something to drink with breakfast in the morning, or after richer meals, when it's cold and damp outside, or something fresh and aromatic in the springtime. Coffee has such a diverse range of exciting and interesting flavours once we go beyond strong, mild, smooth, bitter. Enjoy your journey.

EXTRACTION: STRENGTH AND FLAVOUR

Your choice of brewing method may be down to the style of cup you prefer (such as a short intense serving of espresso, or a long mug of clear delicate filtered coffee), or the amount of ritual or preparation you enjoy. It also depends upon how strong, intense or full-bodied a cup you prefer.

The word 'strong' needs a bit of understanding first. In our world, strength refers to the ratio of coffee grounds to water. For most coffee drinkers, however, the term is used to describe the sense of bitterness or roast intensity, with darker roasts being perceived as stronger, and lighter roasts as milder. This scale has become a requirement for UK companies wishing to sell through supermarket retailers, with a numbered 'strength guide' on the front of the pack. However, if used to compare two similar roasts of different coffees given the same brewing, this designator can be a blunt tool, and with subjective opinion or personal taste can even be slightly misleading. Here's why.

Extraction is the process at the heart of brewing, and as the term suggests it means taking some elements out of the grounds and into the water. Most of the content of ground coffee isn't actually wanted in the cup. Only about 25 per cent by weight is soluble; the rest is mostly cellulose fibre – which does not dissolve.

Within that 25 per cent lies a range of compounds that carry all of the aromatic and taste elements of the coffee, but not all are positive. For the best balance of flavours, we actually only want around 18 to 22 per cent extracted from the grounds and into the brew. Less than 18 per cent and the coffee can taste

sour, thin and lifeless; more than around 22 per cent and the flavours are compacted and astringent. The most commonly experienced over-extraction of coffee flavour comes from badly made espresso (Americanos, usually), where too much water passes through the small amount of grounds and takes everything it can; the resulting cup is ashy and bitter. For those who merely seek caffeine, and think it should come with a bitter kick in the pants, it's difficult to move people back to the sweeter, rounded, gentle side of coffee. (We live to try, however!)

A shot of espresso coffee extracting perfectly. The thin stream just hangs in a slight curve from the filter spouts and is as thin as a mouse tail (coda di topo).

The best brewing method to think about when trying to understand the process is a simple filter. Anyone who has made a pot of filter coffee has seen that as the brew begins to emerge from the bottom of the filter holder, for the first minute or two the liquid is dark, almost syrupy; if tasted it would be too intense, with no real flavours being discerned. This is the extraction stage and it continues as water flows over the grounds, washing all of the compounds into the pot. After the first couple of minutes, the stream becomes paler as less extractable material remains within the grounds. This is the dilution phase of the brew. Liquid continues to pass through the grounds, but by now it's mainly water, which dilutes the intense flavouring material already extracted to a palatable concentration.

If too much water has been loaded into the filter machine or poured over, some extraction will continue and the bitter or astringent compounds will then form a higher percentage of the overall brew – and the resulting cup quality falls. If you seek a milder cup, less strong, the best advice is to brew at full strength and then add water directly into the pot or cup, as this reduces the concentration of coffee without drawing further from the grounds.

The most direct way to control extraction is through correct grinding of the coffee beans. Put simply, the finer the grind, the more surface area will be open to the water, and finer particles will give up their contents more quickly into the brew. Brewing methods requiring longer contact time, such as cafetière (French press), need a coarser grind so as not to over-extract the flavours.

Time is another factor and for most methods (apart from espresso) a total brew time of between three and five minutes will produce the perfect cup. The time factor comes into play because the various compounds within the coffee extract at different rates. Generally the sugars and complex aromatics are extracted within the first couple of minutes, the more bitter compounds building gradually and peaking at around five to seven minutes. So it's a good idea for brewing to be completed by this time.

At the opposite end of the spectrum is under-extraction, which often yields a less offensive but equally unpalatable brew. Espresso demonstrates this when the grind is too coarse, allowing the water to pass through the grounds too quickly and without picking up the good stuff on its way into the cup. The serving will not have the foam-like crema on

Perfect shot of espresso with reddish-brown, evenly coloured crema that persists on top of the serving.

the surface, and will taste thin and watery, and probably sour or even salty. Filter coffee will result in similar under-extraction when the grind is too coarse. In the case of a cafetière, under-extraction occurs when the plunger is pushed down after only a minute or so.

Having seen that extraction and strength are different, the next question is: how much coffee should we use? Interestingly, opinion on this varies around the world (and also with degree of roast). In recent years, investigations using blind-tasting panels have shown that for most UK and US consumers, a coffee-to-water ratio of around 60g per litre of water will be appropriate. The gold medal for the strongest brews goes to the Nordic countries, with around 90g per litre the preferred strength. Must be something to do with the dark winters!

GRINDING

Getting the right grind for any brewing method is important because it determines how quickly the water passes over the grounds. This is commonly referred to as contact time. A simple rule of thumb says that the shorter the brew time, the finer the grind. Which seems obvious when you think about this: when the coffee and water spend little time together, the coffee must be ground very fine to open up as much surface area as possible to allow the flavours, oils and volatile elements to be extracted quickly.

To illustrate this, take two examples. At one end of the spectrum is the cafetière, also known as a French press, which uses a medium–coarse grind. If the grounds were very fine, it would be difficult to press down the screen as water couldn't move through the tightly packed puck of grounds. To compensate for the larger size of the medium–coarse grind, we allow a longer brew time – around 4 minutes.

At the other end of the spectrum is espresso, in which the water is forced through the grounds in just 20–30 seconds. This means that the grind must be very fine to allow quick extraction of flavour. It's very difficult to push the water through – but espresso machines pump the water through the grounds under high pressure.

For coarser grinds it's possible to get up close and to see, with a little experience, how lumpy or gritty the coffee particles are. For finer grinds such as espresso, it's better to rub them between your fingers – they may feel like fine flour, coarse flour or even fine polenta, and you may feel a little grittiness.

There are two types of coffee grinder, burr and blade, but if you're serious about coffee, only a burr grinder will do. A burr grinder works rather like a millstone, grinding the coffee beans between two discs; by changing the distance between the discs it can achieve different grind sizes to match your brewing method and will grind your coffee beans evenly. Blade grinders slice, rather than grind, and can't achieve the uniformity of grind size that's needed for precise brewing in each method.

Burr grinders are available in the kitchen electricals department of many culinary and department stores or online. Most of these grinders will have multiple settings, from very fine to coarse, so you can use them for any brewing method and they will give consistent results from brew to brew.

Manually operated grinders, where one of the burrs is attached to a crank handle and the grounds are collected in a glass or plastic chamber below the burrs, have become popular among the coffee geekdom. As long as the burrs are correctly adjusted these provide the same consistency as electric models and are smaller and more portable – and fun if you want an aromatic workout before brewing your morning cup. When travelling in producing countries, a hand grinder and an AeroPress are essential kit to ensure that we always have a great cup of coffee to drink, even in the remotest villages.

Facing page: Burrs over blades. Burrs achieve a much more even consistency of grind than blades, which roughly chop the beans. Below: Two burr grinders: a hand-powered manual grinder (left) and an electric-operated version (right). Manual grinding is very satisfying but electric models are easier to adjust for different brewing needs.

The following explanations of grinds are intended as close approximations. Try experimenting with small changes of grind, coarser and finer, while using the same coffee and water: this can make a significant difference to the cup. Too fine can lead to over-extraction and harsh, bitter flavours; too coarse can result in under-extracted coffee with a thin, dull or even woody aspect.

TURKISH GRIND (EXTREMELY FINE)

Almost like icing sugar (confectioners' sugar) or fine milled flour. In the Turkish brewing method, ground coffee is boiled with sugar and water and forms a thick suspension that settles to the bottom of the cup or glass after pouring. Many domestic electric grinders will struggle to get grounds this fine; a manual grinder may yield best results.

ESPRESSO GRIND (VERY FINE)

The finest grind in everyday use is that for espresso brewing. The idea of espresso is to get maximum flavour and oil extraction into a very small volume of water in a short time. The coffee needs to be very finely ground, like powder, but with a very fine grittiness when rubbed between the fingers.

AEROPRESS GRIND (MEDIUM–FINE)

This manual, almost espresso-style brewing method brews in a short time, around 30 seconds of stirring after pouring the water in before pushing the plunger down. A medium–fine grind, similar to caster (superfine) sugar, is needed.

CAFETIÈRE GRIND (MEDIUM–COARSE)

Cafetière brewing requires that the plunger be pushed down without too much resistance, otherwise the glass carafe is at risk of breaking. As the contact time is fully under our control, we use a coarser grind to make plunging easy and compensate by extending the contact time to around 4 minutes. This means a medium–coarse grind, the grain size a little larger than demerara sugar.

FILTER GRIND (MEDIUM–FINE)

Whether a manual pour-over filter or an electric filter machine is used, a medium–fine grind similar to caster (superfine) sugar is needed to give a little resistance to the water being poured into the filter basket. While the entire brew will take 4–6 minutes, our view of the contact time is more about each drop rather than the total volume. Each drop will pass through the filter quite quickly and the grind must strike a balance between resistance and open surface area. If it's too fine, the coffee can over-extract and even overflow the filter basket. Too coarse and the coffee will taste thin and under-extracted, regardless of how much is put into the filter.

BREWING METHODS

For some people, brewing coffee is an almost spiritual event. They get profound pleasure from the whole ritual of weighing the beans, grinding the coffee, adding water to the grounds and watching it bubble up, releasing the pent-up aromas. They love the wait – and the aromas – while the coffee is brewing. For others, brewing is the second greatest cause for anxiety (after choosing which coffee to buy). It's an issue that unfortunately gets in the way of a common shared experience: brewing can result in your tasting exactly what we'd hoped for, or disappointment – for us as well as you!

Brewing nightmares also affect our professional world and cause us, as a company, real heartache. As a roaster supplying most of our trade customers in cafés, restaurants and hotels, we rarely get through a week where we don't get a call from one outlet or other with a comment that 'something's wrong with this week's coffee' or 'your blend or roast has changed.' We go to huge lengths checking, tasting and understanding our coffees to ensure that what goes out the door every day is what we want it to be, and we spend a lot of time with our customers teaching them how to use their espresso or other kit so that they get the right result. When we get such a call, we always visit or speak to them to check that the equipment is clean and correctly set up, because small changes can make a huge difference in the final brew. In the café or restaurant, people very rarely blame the person who made it; so it's our reputation at risk.

Some people think that espresso and its milky derivatives are the 'best' coffee. Professionals don't think that way. They know espresso is just one of many styles, and personal choice plays a key part. At home, we usually both start the day with filtered brews which are more gentle on the palate: taste is most sensitive early in the day and a cup of filtered coffee can often contain more caffeine than a shot of espresso (for those who also need the kick out of bed).

We would recommend trying to brew espresso only after you've learned to understand methods such as pour-over filters or cafetière. Brewed coffee may seem simpler than espresso, but it can go seriously wrong if you don't master the fundamentals of whatever method you're using.

In the following section we'll explore the dos and don'ts for various brewing methods. Always remember that coffee brewing is highly personal. Each set of brewing tools is different. Our brewing methods are based on our own equipment, which might differ from yours. So these aren't rules – they're guidelines. Good taste is subjective. So it's not about what we think your brew should taste like. It's about whether you like the taste. Have a fiddle with the measurements, grind coarseness, and extraction times to create your perfect cup.

GETTING IT RIGHT, FROM THE START

There are two common problems with brewed coffee. One, not using enough coffee. In each of the methods described in the following pages we've suggested the amount of coffee (weighed in grams) that we've found to give the best results. Two, the coffee is ground too coarse or too fine for the method used.

Many people think that they should pour the water over the ground beans immediately after it's come to the boil. This isn't right. The water should be just off the boil, and the ideal temperature is generally 94°C/202°F. Use a thermometer if you want to be accurate and consistent; alternatively, just wait for a few moments, until the sound of boiling water in your kettle has subsided.

Equipment

To make coffee at home you need some form of brewing equipment. There are three items that we regard as useful, bordering on essential. For a fresh, balanced, and perfectly poured cup, we recommend all three.

1 A good coffee grinder

The (not-so-secret) secret behind a great cup of coffee is a great grinder. If you seriously want to get serious about coffee, you have to buy whole beans and grind them. Whole beans stay flavourful longer than ground coffee, which starts to lose its delicious aroma just 15 minutes after grinding. For the ideal brew, you'll want to grind your coffee just before you're ready to brew.

We recommend using a burr grinder – but a blade grinder is better than no grinder. Oh, and use it only for coffee. Grinders can grind nuts and spices too, but those flavours will stick around in the machine and contaminate your brew.

2 Scales

Many people brewing at home use a measuring spoon to measure their coffee. Professionals use digital scales. These should measure in 2g increments (or smaller: many affordable kitchen scales now measure in 1g increments), and you may already own these if you're a keen cook. Digital scales aren't a necessity if you're just starting out. But as you get more serious about perfecting your brewing methods, they'll become essential. Exact weights of ground coffee and water – yes, water – produce exact results. Some digital kitchen scales have a setting that measures water volume by weight, but it's easy if you remember that 1 millilitre (ml) of water weighs 1 gram (g). You'll get a more accurate result if you weigh it on scales rather than in a measuring jug.

3 A good kettle

Kettles are used for boiling water. So is there much difference between one kettle and another? In the case of gooseneck kettles, there most definitely is. These kettles have long S-shaped spouts which enable you to pour with far greater control than ordinary domestic kettles. We use the Hario kettle, manufactured by the makers of the V60 brewing systems. A Hario kettle looks a bit like a miniature watering can with a long, thin spout. This makes controlling the flow and placement of water more exact. It also looks super cool. You don't absolutely have to have one – but your brewing life will be much easier if you do.

OTHER EQUIPMENT

Not quite as critical but still very good to have.

Timer
The one on your oven or microwave will be fine – as long as it can be used without turning on the oven. But a small digital timer is cheap to buy, and you can keep it by your brewing equipment.

Thermometer
A digital instant-read probe thermometer is the best kind. (It's also useful for cooking.)

Water filter
There are often good reasons to buy a water filter (see pages 89–91).

POUR OVER (V60)

Simple, clean, accessible. If you're just getting into coffee, drip brewing is a great place to start. You'll probably have seen someone using a hand-brew dripper before – an inverted cone-shaped funnel slowly draining extracted coffee through a filter. This single-cup brewing method is commonplace in coffee houses around the world, and produces a delicate and sophisticated cup.

Result   A clean, light- to medium-bodied brew
Good for... When you only want a single, tasty cup

You'll need

V60 (or similar filter cone)

Filter paper

Dose: 15g
Brew water: 250g (ml)
Water temp: 94°C
Overall brew time: 2½ minutes
Grind size: Medium–fine

Method

1 Fold your paper filter along the seam and open it out into a cone. Put the cone into your V60 (which should be sitting on top of a cup or jug).

2 Rinse the filter by pouring hot water through it and into the cup, then discard the water.

3 Place your pre-measured ground coffee in the filter paper and level it out with a gentle shake.

4 Put your V60 and cup (or jug) on the scales and set to zero.

5 Start the timer, then slowly pour 50g of the water into the coffee, saturating all the grounds and making them bloom, or swell.

6 After 30 seconds pour in 100g more water. Pour in concentric circles into the coffee itself (not the sides of the filter paper).

7 After 60 seconds, pour in 50g more water.

8 At 90 seconds, add another 50g water. (All of your water (250g) should be in by the 90-second mark.)

9 Now, let it drip until finished, which should take an additional 30–90 seconds.

10 If it's taking longer to finish than expected, coarsen the grind next time. If it's running short, try a finer grind.

FILTER PAPERS

These are available in a variety of sizes and commonly either as bleached (whitened) or unbleached.

The size of filter paper needed is determined by the coffee maker used; some types have recommended papers manufactured to fit without needing to cut or resort to origami. The most widely available filters are the Melitta-style shape made for electric filter machines; they have a straight base rather than a perfect cone shape. Cone-shaped papers are used for the Hario V60 and other 'drippers' of this style and are best sought from specialist coffee retailers.

Like any paper product, filter papers are made from wood pulp and contain cellulose and starches that leach into the brew and give a musty, papery flavour to the coffee. Papers that have been whitened will have significantly fewer of these and yield better-tasting coffee. Chlorine was for a long time used as a bleaching agent, but from an environmental point of view it's not a good idea to use lots of chlorine to bleach papers. Oxygen-whitened papers are now widely available; these use hydrogen peroxide to bleach the paper and remove the pulpy flavour; after use, hydrogen peroxide breaks down into water and oxygen.

Whichever type of paper is used, we always recommend rinsing the filter paper through with hot water before brewing the coffee. To find out just how much of an effect this makes, take two mugs of boiled water, add a filter paper to one and leave for 3–4 minutes, then taste them both. You will definitely notice a difference – and remember that water makes up 98 per cent of your cup of coffee.

POUR OVER (CHEMEX)

This contraption, looking rather like a wine decanter, is the wonderfully charming Chemex. It was invented by Peter Schlumbohm in 1941, and the design has remained largely unchanged. It's great for entertaining because it can make a lot of coffee – and look good while doing it.

It's made in various sizes: the smallest is described as '3 cup', which makes two decent-sized mugs. It's highly recommended to use the specially designed Chemex filter papers, which you can buy from specialist coffee retailers.

Result   A clean, light- to medium-bodied brew
Good for… Dinner parties and impressing friends or when want to drink 2–4 cups

You'll need

Chemex (the '3-cup' model will make enough for 1–2 mugs)

Chemex filter paper

Dose: 25g
Brew water: 400g (ml)
Water temp: 94°C
Overall brew time: 4 minutes
Grind size: Medium

Method

1 The Chemex filter paper comes as a large square or round sheet that is folded twice into quarters. Open out the folded paper so that there is a single layer on one side and three on the other. Place the triple-layered section of the filter paper on the spout side of the glass jar where a deep channel is formed in the glass. This allows the correct rate of flow out from the upper chamber.

2 Rinse the filter by pouring hot water through it, then discard the water.

3 Place your pre-measured ground coffee in the filter paper and level it out with a gentle shake.

4 Start the timer, then slowly pour 50ml of the water into the coffee, saturating all the grounds.

5 After 30 seconds, pour in 150ml more water.

6 At 90 seconds, add another 200ml water. (All your water (400ml) should be in by the 90-second mark.) Now, let it drip until finished.

7 After 4 minutes, your brew should be good to go.

8 If your brew is taking longer than expected, coarsen the grind next time. If it's running short, try a finer grind.

CAFETIÈRE (FRENCH PRESS)

Ah, the trusty old cafetière (French for 'coffee maker'), also known as the French press. The design was first patented by an Italian designer in 1929 but was modified by another designer, Faliero Bondanini, and patented again in 1958. Some people swear by them. They come in a range of sizes, from single serving to party size (12 cups) and they do have the virtue of being self-contained and compact: the only equipment you need is the cafetière itself. The most common size is the '8-cup' model, but remember that this refers to small, espresso-type cups: if you're pouring mugs you'll get three servings. Use 7–9g ground coffee per 'cup'; for an 8-cup model, 55–60g coffee will be strong enough for most tastes.

Result   A heavier body than filter coffee and a complex flavour profile
Good for... A great place to start brewing coffee at home

You'll need

Large cafetière (the '8-cup' model will make enough for 3 mugs)

Dose: 55g
Brew water: 850g (ml)
Water temp: 94°C
Overall brew time: 4 minutes
Grind size: Medium–coarse

Method

1 Preheat your cafetière by pouring in some boiling water and giving it a swirl.

2 Discard the water, then put in your pre-measured ground coffee.

3 Pour some just-off-boiling water over the coffee to saturate all the grounds, then slowly pour in the rest of the measured water.

4 Let it steep for 4 minutes, with the plunger cap on, but not pressed down (that'll stop the heat escaping).

5 Remove the plunger, then stir three times with a spoon.

6 Replace the plunger, and carefully plunge at a slow, steady pace.

7 For best results, don't let the brewed coffee sit on its grounds for more than a few minutes.

AEROPRESS

The AeroPress is a relative newbie in the coffee game. It's an innovative, manually powered little gadget that's a cheap, effective way of making a great espresso-like brew. Our method is a hack. It's a little more complicated than the standard modus operandi, but it's cleaner and significantly more controlled.

Result   A medium-bodied brew with a relatively complex flavour profile
Good for... A cheap, low-maintenance coffee maker, great for coffee on the go

You'll need

AeroPress

The quantities below are for a double shot, or a drink diluted to 250ml
Dose: 15g
Brew water: 250g (ml)
Water temp: 94°C
Overall brew time: 2 minutes
Grind size: Medium–fine

Method

1 Place a filter paper in the AeroPress cap and secure it to the body.

2 Place the body over your cup, with the cap down.

3 Flush the contraption with hot water. This will preheat the vessel and rinse the filter paper. Empty the water from your cup.

4 Put your pre-measured ground coffee in the AeroPress body.

5 Pour in the water, saturating all the grounds.

6 Gently stir the coffee inside the Aeropress body for 20–30 seconds.

7 At an angle, carefully insert the plunger. Once it's in, pull it up slightly to create a vacuum.

8 Let it steep for another 30–60 seconds before starting to plunge. You might have to push a little – be careful with the cup below – push straight down, being careful not to push to one side and spill all over the counter! The extraction should take around 30 seconds.

9 If the coffee is too strong, next time stir and steep for a slightly shorter time. If the coffee lacks body or character, steep for slightly longer.

STOVETOP

Stovetop coffee makers, also known as moka pots, are great for lots of reasons. They're cheap, compact and simple. If you're vigilant, these little contraptions can produce an exquisite, intense coffee comparable to espresso made on a fancy machine. But take your eye off the ball and it'll burn. Quickly.

The bottom part of this screw-together coffee maker holds the water. Coffee is placed in a container (the basket) which sits inside the bottom pot, and then the upper section is screwed on. When heated, water rises up through a central spout and infuses through the coffee. The brewed coffee continues upwards through a column at the centre of the upper pot and is collected there. A stovetop moka pot makes a small volume of brewed coffee with a high ratio of grounds and can offer some of the body that espresso provides.

Result   A heavy-bodied intense brew
Good for... Traditionalist coffee drinkers

You'll need

Stovetop/moka pot

A heat source (electric or gas stove)

Oven gloves or folded tea towels

Dose: 15g
Brew water: 250g (ml)
Water temp: 94–96°C
Overall brew time: approx. 2 minutes
Grind size: Medium–fine

Method

1 Bring a kettle of water to the boil.

2 Remove the top section of the moka pot and the basket. Fill the bottom pot with hot water from your kettle, making sure the level is below the safety valve.

3 Put your ground coffee into the coffee basket and level it out with a gentle shake, without patting it down.

4 Put the basket into the bottom pot, with the spout facing down.

5 Screw the top section onto the bottom pot. Careful, it'll be hot.

6 Put the pot over a low to medium heat.

7 When the pot starts gurgling, your coffee's good to go. Take it off the heat – carefully, as it will be hot – and serve.

 TOP TIP

FILLING WITH HOT WATER MAKES THE PROCESS QUICKER AND AVOIDS BAKING THE COFFEE WHILE THE POT HEATS UP.

SYPHON

Beautiful. Complicated. Otherworldly. Syphons have been around for almost 200 years and produce clear, consistent, sediment-free coffee. They can be a little tricky to master, but hey – being a steampunk takes work, right? Never seen a syphon brewer before? Then check this out. Note that to use this method you need a burner or a halogen lamp. If you're not inclined to mess with either of those things, sidestep the syphon and use another method.

Result   A visually exciting experience, with a clean and complex flavour range.
Good for... Scientists and coffee geeks

You'll need

Syphon

Spirit burner (or other heat source, such as a butane-filled micro burner similar to a mini camping stove)

Dose: 20g
Brew water: 300g (ml)
Water temp: 91–94°C
Overall brew time: 2½ minutes
Grind size: Medium–fine

Method

1 Remove the lid and upper chamber from the syphon. Make sure that the filter assembly is securely fitted inside the upper chamber with the chain running through the tube below and hooked onto its rim. Rinse the filter through with hot water, add the pre-measured ground coffee and stand in the inverted holder/lid. Add 300ml of hot water to the lower globe chamber.

2 Using the burner, heat the water in the bottom bowl until it just begins to reach a gentle simmer. You may need to reduce the flame to avoid rapid boiling.

3 Gently and carefully place the top chamber into the neck of the lower bowl until it forms a seal. The water will rise to meet the coffee in the upper chamber. Stir the coffee in the top bowl to ensure it is fully and completely wetted. Turn the flame down or move the burner a little out from under the syphon so that just enough heat is maintained to keep the water in the top for around 1–2 minutes.

4 Remove or extinguish the burner and the suction created will pull the brewed coffee back down into the lower chamber.

5 Gently remove the top chamber, stand it again in the holder/lid while it cools.

6 Serve your coffee from the lower chamber or transfer into a serving jug to cool slightly before serving.

 TOP TIP

DRAW-DOWN TOO FAST (I.E. FASTER THAN 30 SECONDS)? YOUR GRIND WAS PROBABLY TOO COARSE: TRY AGAIN WITH A FINER GRIND. WATER LEFT IN THE TOP BULB? GO COARSER. HAVE A PLAY UNTIL YOU GET IT JUST RIGHT.

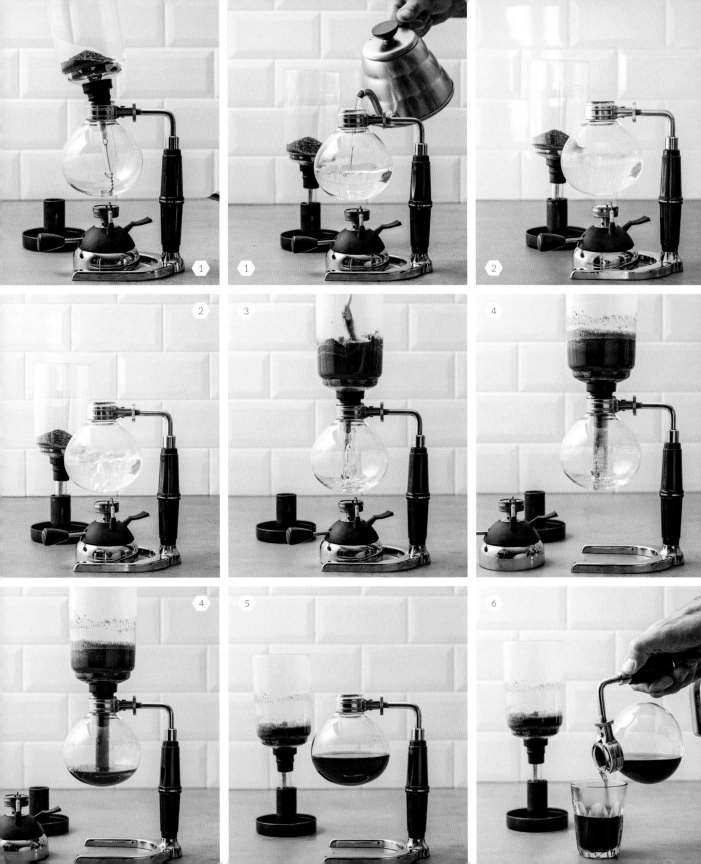

COLD BREW

Cold brew? It must be summer. Sunshine, soaring temperatures, and time for a cube of ice (or three). Cold brew coffee requires a little foresight because of the extended steeping time, but it's definitely worth it. There are two methods, the cold dripper (pictured) or the less fancy but much more easily repeatable immersion method as described below. Both methods produce a naturally sweeter cup and a softer acidity compared to hot brewed coffee of the same origin or type. Cold brew coffee keeps for two weeks. The grounds absorb a certain amount of water, so this method will make around 750ml of chilled coffee.

Result   A light-bodied, delicate brew with high clarity of flavour
Good for... A way to start to understand the subtle nuances of speciality coffee

You'll need

120g coffee

Muslin cloth

Kitchen string

Large jug

1 litre fresh filtered water

Dose: Brew at double strength, around 120–140g per litre of water to be used. This gives a strong brew good to be served over ice
Overall brew time: Around 12 hours
Grind size: Medium-coarse

Method

1 Grind your coffee to a coarse, cafetière-like grind. Maybe even a little coarser.

2 Place the coffee in the muslin cloth and tie the top with kitchen string to make a large 'coffee bag'.

3 Put the water into a large jug and put the bag into the water. Give it a little knead and shake to make sure all of the coffee is saturated.

4 Give it some time and patience. It needs to brew at room temperature for 10–16 hours. Works well overnight.

5 Wake up. Rush to the kitchen. Remove the bag and give it a squeeze.

6 For best results, bottle the coffee by pouring through a rinsed paper filter to remove some of the sediment that may have collected in the bottom of the brew.

7 Check the fridge to make sure the coffee is cold enough – and also that there's plenty of cold beer in there alongside it.

8 Light up the barbecue.

The cold dripper pictured here uses ice melting to slowly and almost painfully slowly drip cold water over the grounds held in a bottomless glass jar below. Instead of a base, the jar has a metal filter that allows the water as it slowly percolates through the grounds to drip through and be collected in a glass jug below. The ice container also has a tiny adjustable valve to regulate the speed of the drip through. When correctly set up, it should take around 12 hours to brew.

ESPRESSO

It all sounds so simple. Very hot water is forced through ground coffee under pressure to make a small volume of thick, well textured, intensely flavourful liquid. That's what espresso is. You heat the water nearly to boiling point, then force it through a measured dose of grounds contained in a shallow cylindrical cup called a portafilter. (The dimensions of the cup explain why the dose is often called a 'puck'.) The pressure needed to force the water through is tremendous: somewhere around 9 bars, or 130 pounds per square inch. That huge pressure forces through far more of the beans' content, especially oils and dissolved solids, than you get in other brewing methods. One result of that is the much-prized crema, the foam on top of a well-made espresso.

But if it seems simple in principle, remember that appearances can be deceiving. There is a huge volume of technical and scientific literature on the subject of espresso. The variables at every stage of making the drink are numerous and complex, and even the smallest change in any one of them can profoundly affect the quality of the drink. This is one reason that the coffee professionals called baristas, those who make espresso in cafés, coffee bars and all the other places where the drink is served, acquire an almost religious zeal for their art. This section explores espresso from its origins to its everyday incarnation in hundreds of thousands of tiny cups all around the globe.

THE HISTORY OF ESPRESSO

Espresso seems such a quintessential part of Italian culture – and increasingly of world culture – that it may come as a shock to learn it is a relatively new drink. Espresso coffee means coffee made speedily and to order, and the dream of producing it reliably has been around for over a century.

But the first espresso as we know it did not arrive on the world stage until 1948. This places the fascination with Italian café culture – a fixture of films and books in the 1950s and 1960s – in context. Those beatniks and boulevardiers were in love with a drink that had only just been invented.

Espresso arose in response to a problem that was driven more by commercial needs than by the desire for better coffee. Brewing coffee by most conventional methods takes quite a lot of time: at least five minutes and sometimes much longer. You can brew it in batches and hold it over the heat, but as anyone who's had a noontime cup of coffee from the 10 o'clock brew on the office machine can tell you, the resulting cup is more pain than pleasure. If your customers are waiting impatiently for coffee on their way to work, keeping them standing for ten minutes is not a great sales ploy.

The 19th century is sometimes called the age of steam because of all the technical advances wrought by steam power, and it was steam that inventors turned to for fast coffee. The first patent was granted in 1884 to a businessman and inventor in Turin named Angelo Moriondo, who owned a café. His was the first steam-powered espresso machine, but he didn't develop it further. The next important steps came in 1901, when a Milanese named Luigi Bezzera introduced (and patented the following year) several improvements to the machine. Two of these in particular were important: the groupheads and the portafilters that fitted into them with a little 'puck' of ground coffee through which water would be forced under pressure. Both features still lie at the heart of modern espresso machines.

Below: Bar Moka, opened in Soho (London) in 1953. The design could be duplicated today and still look modern. Facing page (top left): 1959 advertisement for Caffé Reggio in New York City, showing its famous 1902 espresso machine; (top right) No time to stop: the need for speedy service drove the quest for perfect espresso right from the start; (below) The Caffé Reggio espresso machine in use, 1942. This picture was taken by Marjory Collins, a photographer working for the US government's Office of War Information, as part of a project documenting everyday American life.

CAFFÉ REGGIO

ORIGINAL - CAPPUCCINO

119 McDOUGAL STREET
NEW YORK 12
Telephone: GRamercy 5-9557

Open Every Day – From 1:00 P. M. – 2:00 A. M.
Friday and Saturday – From 12 Noon – 3:30 A. M.

Bezzera lacked the ability (or perhaps just money) to get his machines made on an industrial scale. But another Milanese, Desiderio Pavoni, bought the patents and started manufacturing in Milan – working with Bezzera – in 1905. His company was called La Pavoni, and both his name and Bezzera's survive to this day as espresso-machine manufacturers.

The early machines had some limitations, which would make them less than popular with today's drinkers. The water was heated with open fire, so smoky flavours could get into the brew. And the pressure inside the great metal domes of these machines was far lower than that in modern machines: perhaps 2 bars as opposed to 9 bars.

But that seems not to have mattered, because espresso had reached the essential point of development: it could be made and consumed quickly. Its popularity spread not just in Italy but throughout Europe, and it travelled with Italians who went to live in other parts of the world. The Caffè Reggio in Manhattan's Greenwich Village opened in 1927 and still has its original espresso machine, dating from 1902. (The owner, Domenico Parisi, is also said to have introduced the cappuccino to the USA.) Illycaffè, a company that's still prominent in the market today, launched in 1933, focussing on selling espresso beans – the founder, Francesco Illy, also invented a coffee machine.

Above: Twin sisters demonstrate a two-lever Gaggia espresso machine in London, 1958. Right: Drive-by brewing: an early advertisement for Bezzera, founded in 1901 by an engineer who patented improvements on Angelo Moriondo's original machine.

Espresso as we know it came into being when the Milanese Achille Gaggia introduced his revolutionary machine in 1948. Gaggia's machine (they're still made today) heated the water in a small boiler and then forced it into an even smaller space, with a capacity that was just the size of a shot of espresso. The barista pulled a lever (hence 'pulling a shot') that let the water out under nine atmospheres of pressure. It made each shot the same size. And because of the enormous pressure, the machine extracted compounds that produced the famous crema – brownish-tan foam – that we still expect from a properly made espresso.

Gaggia's machines were much smaller than their predecessors, and thus easier to transport. With that one giant lever-driven step forward, Gaggia paved the way for an even more extensive espresso diaspora in Europe and the USA. Gaggia's great achievement was followed in 1961 by the introduction of the Faema E61: here the lever was replaced by a motorized pump, and water came directly from the mains, rather than an internal boiler. This simplified the pulling of a shot, as all the barista had to do was push a button to get the process under way.

Needless to say, there have been innumerable advances in espresso machines since 1961. Get two coffee geeks in the same room and you will hear all about them. In the 'third wave' of coffee appreciation, fanaticism about hardware and production details has become a feature of coffee bars from Sydney to Stockholm. But in the end, the machine is no better than the barista who's working it. This is a constant in the history of espresso.

ESPRESSO MACHINE METHOD

The traditional espresso machine. Available in an array of aesthetically pleasing designs. Moustached barista optional. If you're lucky enough to have a full-fledged espresso machine to experiment on, making minor adjustments to any of the steps below will affect the fullness, richness and intensity of the cup. You can have endless hours of fun on one of these clever machines.

Result   A deep, concentrated, intense coffee. Also great with milk.
Good for... Making coffee shop-style drinks in the home. For the serious investor.

You'll need

A good quality espresso machine and
a hand-held tamp tool

A quality burr grinder (optional, but highly
recommended)

Freshly ground coffee

Measuring scales (recommended). Small
differences of weight can be difficult to see
but make a big difference to the end result

Dose: 17–19g
Brew water: 28–36g (ml)
Water temp: 91–96°C
Overall brew time: 22–30 seconds
Grind size: Very fine

Method

1 Remove the portafilter from the grouphead
– twist from right to left until it dislodges.

2 Flush the grouphead for 2–3 seconds.

3 Empty the portafilter (if it isn't already
empty) and wipe to make sure there isn't any
leftover residue or moisture.

4 Measure out your coffee: use scales for exact results.

5 Put the coffee in the portafilter, level it out with a light shake or
a dosing tool.

6 Tamp the coffee: use a hand tamper to firmly compress the grounds
and level them out. This will force out any air pockets and create a longer
extraction process. The grounds must be level to ensure even extraction.

7 Clean the rim of the portafilter and spouts, and flush the
grouphead again.

8 Lock the portafilter into the grouphead by twisting it from left
to right, and select the cup.

9 As soon as the portafilter is in, start the water flow. You should have
3–5 seconds to put the cup under the spouts before the flow starts.

10 Keep an eye on the extraction time of your espresso – this will vary
according to taste.

11 When your espresso's poured, stop the water flow.

TOP TIP

KEEP YOUR MACHINE AND ALL ITS
COMPONENTS CLEAN. IT'LL KEEP YOUR
ESPRESSO CRISP AND UNBLEMISHED.

TAMPING

It might seem like a relatively unimportant step to devote so much attention to tamping but this stage of the espresso process is one of the most important aspects in getting consistent shots from your machine. This compacting of the grounds provides resistance to the water flowing through and ensures that all of the coffee grounds extract evenly.

1 Start with a clean and dry portafilter. Grounds from your last brew will cause over-extracted, bitter flavours in the serving.

2 Dose the ground coffee from the grinder directly into the portafilter if it has an adjustable timer function, or weigh the grounds and tip into the portafilter to ensure consistency. Just 1 gram difference can make a significant change to the taste.

3 The grounds may pile up in the filter basket, so gently tap the sides with your hand to settle them down into the basket.

4 Rest the portafilter on a counter. A correctly sized tamp just fits within the basket. Rest this on top of the grounds. Press down with with your body weight over the tamp. Twist the tamp slightly left to right to 'polish' the surface.

5 Before loading into the machine, wipe your hand across the rim of the filter to avoid grounds getting into the seal area, which can allow coffee and water to leak out of the portafilter instead of passing into the cup.

The tamp must be level in the basket to avoid water passing only through the shallower side and not extracting flavours evenly and consistently. Always rest the portafilter on a surface to ensure good pressure is applied. It's impossible to tamp properly when it is all up in the air.

Grind too fine or tamp too hard and the espresso drips out too slowly and flavours over-extract (bitterness).

Grind too coarse or tamp not firm enough, and the espresso comes through too quickly and under-extracts (becoming watery and thin).

Ideal shot pouring was classically referred to in Italy as mouse tail (coda di topo) – which it should resemble in colour and thickness.

THE ESPRESSO MENU

You can transform espresso fundamentally – usually by adding milk or other ingredients. Even if you're familiar with these drinks, it's good to know exactly what they should consist of. Of course, the word 'exactly' has to be taken with a pinch of sugar. Many of these drinks are subject to debate, and local usages can differ from one country (or café) to another.

Caffè Americano This is commonly called Americano and it's simply an espresso with hot water added: it has the same flavour as an espresso but is more dilute. The degree of dilution is determined by the number of espresso shots (usually one or two) and the amount of added water. Properly speaking, the term should be used only for drinks where water is poured over the espresso. If that order is reversed, the drink is called a long black. A long black, unlike an Americano, will have some crema on top.

Caffè latte Almost universally referred to simply as latte, this is an espresso with steamed milk. The proportion of milk to coffee can vary considerably, but there is always much more milk – at least twice and sometimes five times as much. It is similar to cappuccino in many respects but has very little foam on top. The drink is akin to much of what's served as *café au lait* or *café crème* in France, and *café con leche* in Spain.

Cappuccino This is made by adding hot textured milk and milk foam to espresso, usually in a large cup with the foam peeping over the top and often dusted with cocoa powder. A cappuccino has a large volume of foam relative to the quantity of milk (the competition standard is 1cm of milk and 1.5cm of foam), and the foam can be worked by the barista to form pictures or patterns in the same way as a latte. Even though we think of it as a quintessentially Italian drink, it probably has its origins in Vienna. The name comes from the brown colour of the robes of the Capuchin order of monks.

Cortado This variant from the Iberian peninsula is 'cut' (*cortado*) with milk in a ratio of up to two parts milk to one part coffee. The milk is hot but traditionally has little foam.

It has become increasingly popular outside its native territory among people who want a fairly small drink in which the punch of espresso is tempered by milk.

Flat white This popular drink originated in New Zealand in the late 1970s or early 1980s. Its worldwide spread means that there are variations in the recipe, but essentially it is a double shot of espresso with around twice as much milk poured over. What distinguishes it from cappuccino is that the milk is textured but almost foam-free – thus the name 'flat' – and though also similar to a latte, the flat white has a higher ratio of coffee to milk.

Lungo This is an Italian espresso variant made with a greater ratio of water to coffee grounds. This is sometimes called 'stretching' the coffee, which gives rise to the French name for it: *café allongé*.

Macchiato This means 'stained' in Italian, and the drink is an espresso in a small cup with a dash of steamed milk. The milk may be slightly foamy on top, but should not be excessively foamy. In some places, the milk is put in first and the coffee second. A piccolo is a version of the macchiato made with ristretto rather than espresso.

Ristretto Literally 'restricted', ristretto is made like an espresso but with half as much water. It is not simply 'half an espresso', however, as not all the flavour-forming compounds are extracted from the coffee grounds. The flavour profile may be punchier and less bitter, and with higher acidity. A ristretto can be used as the basis for an Americano or long black instead of espresso.

CAFFÈ AMERICANO

2 parts
1 part

CAFFÈ LATTE

thick layer
3 parts
1 part

CAPPUCCINO

1 part
1 part
1 part

CORTADO

1 part
1 part

FLAT WHITE

thin layer
2 parts
1 part

LUNGO

1½ parts

MACCHIATO

thin layer
1 part

RISTRETTO

⅓ part

Key
Espresso
Steamed milk
Microfoam
Hot water

MILK MATTERS

Coffee and milk make a great couple and complement each other seamlessly. If you're one of the millions of people who love milky drinks above all other types of coffee, the quality of the milk, and the way it's treated, are extremely important. With many of these drinks, there's two or even three times as much milk as there is coffee. We are regularly asked four main questions about milk:

FULL-FAT OR SKINNY?

Our answer is simple: stop bargaining with yourself over the shortbread and allow yourself those calories in the milk – they're much more rewarding. It's the butterfat in milk that turns, when heated, from solid fat molecules to a liquid, oily state that enhances the richness of the drink. When foamed for cappuccino, the higher fat content allows the foam to remain silky and moist compared to the drier foam created by semi-skimmed or skimmed milk. By the way, do you know what the difference is between a cappuccino with full-fat milk and semi-skimmed? Around twelve calories. You'd have to drink a lot of cappuccino before the extra calories from whole milk started having an impact on your waistline.

WHY DOES THE BARISTA INSIST ON SERVING MY CAPPUCCINO WARM AND NOT SCALDING HOT?

The answer is about the natural sugars in milk, of which the main one is lactose. This type of sugar becomes more soluble as it's heated, and this is why warm milk tastes sweeter than cold. If it's heated too far, however, the milk will scald and become less sweet. And it may make the coffee taste bitter. Your barista knows what he or she is doing.

WHY DO SOME CARTONS OF MILK STEAM WELL AND OTHERS DON'T?

The important component in milk when steaming is the casein protein content. This makes up around 80 per cent of the milk by weight. If the milk is not fresh, these proteins are degraded by amino acids that form in the milk over a few days. Refrigeration slows this down, but leaving milk out of the fridge for too long can speed up its staling – even though it may still smell and taste fresh. A good coffee bar will always use the freshest milk. If you make milky coffee drinks at home, make sure you follow their example. Don't buy the bigger milk cartons – unless you live with a horde of coffee drinkers and have to make ten or twelve cappuccinos and flat whites every day.

WHAT IF I'M TRYING TO AVOID DAIRY PRODUCTS?

For a variety of reasons some people prefer to avoid dairy products. For these coffee drinkers, other milks are becoming very popular – most notably soy and (more recently) almond. If protein levels are good in these milks, they can produce an adequate foam for cappuccino etc. The flavour of both, in our opinion, is less pleasant in quality coffee compared to the more neutral flavour of 'regular' milk. But if you feel you have a compelling reason to avoid lactose, and are not ready to make the switch to filter or drip-brewed coffee drunk without milk, they're a reasonable option.

Milk steaming

The texture of the milk enhances the coffee's characteristics; using the correct steaming technique will help to produce silky and sweet milk. Full-fat (whole) milk is always preferable: the fat and protein content give a better taste and more stable foam.

The three key stages of steaming milk are **aerating**, **texturing** and **polishing**.

1 Fill your milk jug between one third and two thirds full – to the bottom of the spout.

2 Purge the steam wand to remove any residue.

3 Put the steam wand just under the surface of the milk and slightly off centre. Turn on the steam and listen for the hiss.

4 Gradually move the jug down until you have enough micro foam. This is called stretching, or **aerating**. Don't let the milk reach body temperature!

5 Time to texture. Use the spout as an anchor and move the jug up slightly to force the steam wand down, creating a vortex.

6 When the jug gets a bit too hot to hold, it's at 60–65°C (you should not be able to touch the bottom of the jug for more than 3 seconds). Stop **texturing**.

7 Blast steam through the wand to clean it.

8 Tap your milk jug on the side to remove any surface bubbles, then swirl to mix the foam with the liquid. By this point your milk should be shiny, like wet paint. That's why this stage is called **polishing**.

9 Pour.

Top: When it's right, milk creates a whirlpool and tight microbubble foam. Positioning the jug and the tip of the steam wand nozzle is important in getting the right texture.

Bottom: When it's wrong you'll hear sputtering and see large bubbles form, which break up the foam.

LATTE ART TUTORIAL

With a shot of espresso and a jug of perfectly steamed milk, it's time to discover your inner coffee artist.

Tulip

1 After you have polished your lightly textured milk, take the cup in your non-dominant hand and tilt it towards the jug.

2 Start pouring into the centre of the espresso from a reasonable height so as not to let out any of the micro foam. While pouring, try to mix the milk and crema to create a uniform light brown colour.

3 When the liquid starts to get close to the edge of the cup, move the spout of the jug towards the surface of the drink.

4 When it is almost touching you will notice the white blob start to appear. (This is why you tilt the cup, to enable you to get the micro foam onto the surface of the crema.) Think of the spout of the jug as the nib of a pencil. Start your blob close to the lower edge of the cup and push it towards the centre as you pour. Stop there and pull your jug back up.

5 To add more 'leaves' to your tulip repeat steps 3 and 4, each time placing the new blob behind the others.

6 Repeat to continue adding leaves, all the while remembering that the cup is getting fuller, so less tilting is needed.

7 To make the 'stem' at the end, don't stop pouring; instead, lift the jug up.

8 Push the stream of milk towards the far edge of the cup. Lifting the jug up helps make the stream of liquid milk thinner and easier to 'draw with'.

Rosetta

1 After you have polished your lightly textured milk, take the cup in your non-dominant hand and tilt it towards the jug.

2 Start pouring into the centre of the espresso from a reasonable height so as not to let out any of the micro foam. While pouring, try to mix the milk and crema to create a uniform light brown colour.

3 When the liquid starts to get close to the edge of the cup, move the spout of the jug towards the surface of the drink.

4 When it is almost touching you will notice the white blob start to appear. (This is why you tilt the cup, to enable you to get the micro foam onto the surface of the crema.) Think of the spout of the jug as the nib of a pencil. Start your blob close to the lower edge of the cup and push it towards the centre as you pour. Stop there and pull your jug back up.

5 To pour a rosetta, start your blob in the middle and give your jug a very gentle wiggle: you will notice thin 'leaves' appear.

6 Keep doing this until your cup is nearly full, then move the jug back towards your body, while still gently wiggling.

7 To make a heart shape on top, hold your jug still for a second and you will see a small blob appear. To make a fern shape, go back to step 5.

8 Then in one motion lift your jug up and push the stream of milk back through your pattern towards the far edge of your cup.

COFFEE CULTURE

Coffee is powerful stuff – and we're not talking about its flavour or caffeine content. From its first recorded appearances in history, people have regarded it as something special. It's been seen as a drug, capable of doing both good and evil. And it's been seen also as a force in bringing people together – again, for better or worse depending on who was gathering, and where, and for what reason. We regard coffee shops as places for pleasure and conviviality, but a few centuries ago governments saw them (possibly with good reason) as places where dissent and sedition could brew along with the coffee.

From its origins in Yemen, in the Arabian peninsula, to its spread throughout the world in tens of thousands of cafés and millions of homes, coffee has taken a journey that's intimately bound up with our way of life. This chapter surveys just a small sampling of those cultural manifestations of the bean and its brew. From Africa to Venice to the Central Perk by way of London, Istanbul and Berkeley, California, it's a long and fascinating journey.

THE JOURNEY OF COFFEE

There are competing stories, all of them unproved and almost certainly apocryphal, about the discovery of coffee's unique properties. You can take your pick, but the one most often told is this. In the ninth century, a goatherd named Kaldi on a hillside in Ethiopia noticed that some of the goats in his herd were behaving erratically: jumping about with uncharacteristic energy, and so on. He also noticed that the behaviour occurred after the goats had been munching on the bright red berries of a particular bush growing on the hillside. He tried one of the berries himself and felt stimulated and wakeful. So he tried some more, only this time with semi-skimmed goat's milk and a freshly baked croissant. OK, we made the last part up. But the rest is made up as well. It has been told for so long, and it's such a nice story, that we carry on telling it. The one certain truth in the story is the part about Ethiopia: it was here that coffee plants first grew. Every coffee bean grown anywhere on earth, from Malabar to Mexico, has its origins there.

The bean's early history as a basis for brewing is as murky as the dregs of a Turkish coffee, but it is known that by the beginning of the 15th century it had been exported to the Arabian Peninsula and was used by monks in Sufi monasteries in Yemen. It soon travelled to the cities of Mecca and Medina, and to Cairo, and by the middle of the 16th century the new institution of coffee houses had spread in the Middle East. While you might not immediately see the connection between 16th-century Istanbul and your local café, the earliest coffee houses were places where cultivated gentlemen (yes, always men) gathered for the pursuit of refined conversation. This set the pattern for coffee drinking, which has always been associated with a certain type of sophisticated sociability.

In its early days, however, the authorities associated it with other things, including intoxication. Coffee is a drug. It's a stimulant, like cocaine or methamphetamine. Needless to say, it is not as powerful or destructive in its effects as either of those drugs. But its stimulating properties have made it the object of moralizing anti-coffee campaigners over the centuries. And not only that, the coffee houses were places where free debate took place, and could thus be sources of dangerous dissent. As coffee use spread, Muslim religious leaders and civic authorities made numerous attempts to ban the drink. The same would happen in Europe, where a ban on coffee was demanded by some in the Catholic church around the year 1600. Fortunately it was rejected by Pope Clement VIII, allegedly after taking a sip. In Britain in 1675, Charles II tried to ban coffee houses on the grounds that they were 'the resort of idle and disaffected persons ... [where] diverse false, malicious and scandalous reports are devised and spread abroad, to the defamation of His Majesty's Government.' With coffee, unlike other drugs, the anti-prohibitionists always won out.

Coffee, a world traveller

The magic beans arrived in Europe in the late 16th century, both through trade with the Ottoman Empire and through direct shipments from the Yemeni port of Mocha, a name that has been associated with coffee ever since. In the following century the drink became popular – at least among those who could afford it. The first recorded coffee house in Europe opened in Venice in 1645. In England the first was in Oxford, in 1652; the Queen's Lane coffee house in Oxford (1654) is still in business. The Café Procope in Paris (1686) included Voltaire, Rousseau and Thomas Jefferson among its customers.

The increasing popularity of the new drink meant that there was plenty of money to be made from it. Arabian traders had an early monopoly on the trade in beans, and the growers in Yemen tried hard to protect their bushes. But a Dutch trader named Pieter van der Broecke took coffee plants from Yemen to Amsterdam in 1616, and planted them in greenhouses in the city's botanical gardens. They thrived there, and 40 years later the Dutch planted bushes in India and Ceylon (now Sri Lanka). They switched production to their colonies in Java (another name for ever associated with coffee) and in Suriname, and the Dutch quickly came to dominate the European trade in beans.

Facing page: The port of Mocha in Arabia, now Yemen. A watercolour painted by Royal Navy officer Rupert Kirk in 1831. Above left: A coffee shop in Constantinople, now Istanbul. Above right: London café culture around the turn of the 18th century.

It didn't last, however. French colonists planted trees on Hispaniola, the island that is now the Dominican Republic and Haiti, in 1715, and on the island of Bourbon (now Réunion) in the Indian Ocean shortly after. British planters took bushes to Jamaica in 1730 and Portuguese landowners had established plantations in Brazil by the middle of the 18th century. By the end of the century, coffee was a well-established crop in the Caribbean and South America. Demand was fuelled by the events that led to the American Revolution, which expressed its rebellion in a switch from tea to coffee as the hot beverage of choice. That preference has never wavered, as you'll know if you have ever tried to get a really high-quality cup of tea in the States.

COFFEE IN THE 20TH CENTURY

Two countries are usually seen as pivotal in the coffee market in the 20th century: Italy and the USA. This doesn't mean that they're the biggest consumers per head of population, just that the drink was central to their way of life. In Italy it was (and still is) pre-eminently the tiny cup of espresso consumed in a rush, standing up at a café on the way to work. The espresso machine was invented early in the century but developed and improved under various hands. The greatest development came after World War II, when Achille Gaggia patented a machine that could force water through finer grounds at higher pressure, yielding the 'crema' that espresso-lovers demand, and could also produce a good foam of milk for making a cappuccino.

Above left: No grounds for divorce: this mid-20th-century American advertisement was not the only one to regard the serving of good coffee as one of a wife's sacred duties. Above right: Single women, by contrast, were encouraged to embrace the simpler pleasures of instant. Left: At London's first espresso bar, Bar Moka, the crowd at the counter is almost exclusively male.

In the USA, coffee was a big mug (the average American standard serving was around 9 ounces/250ml) of brewed coffee, often with milk or cream and a spoonful of sugar. Coffee drinking rose steadily for the first six decades of the century, and became embedded in the American way of life. This was the land of free refills, of coffee as a symbol of all that was good and simple and satisfying. In a song written by Irving Berlin in 1932, the dark days of the Great Depression, a group cheers itself up by singing:

> Just around the corner,
> There's a rainbow in the sky.
> So let's have another cup of coffee,
> And let's have another piece of pie.

By the end of the 1930s, 98 per cent of American households drank coffee and the country imported some 70 per cent of the world's beans. Most of this was freshly brewed, though a new interloper – instant coffee – also competed for market share. The French brand Sanka had already established itself from the first decades of the century. Then in 1938, Nescafé, created by the Nestlé corporation following a request from the Brazilian Coffee Institute (which needed a way of dealing with a glut of unsaleable beans), created a somewhat superior version of instant coffee that became one of the most famous brands in the world. In many quarters, however, instant was recognized for what it was: something you drink when you don't have access to real coffee. This is one reason it increased in popularity during and after World War II: GIs carried it in their rations, and in many places the taste persisted.

Good coffee was part of the American birthright, with fear of serving the wrong stuff instilled in American consumers through intimidating – and often revoltingly sexist – advertisements. One TV ad from the 1950s shows a man with a woman over his knee, giving her a hard spanking for 'taking chances on getting flat, stale coffee' to serve him at home. Another, from the mid-1960s, shows a woman smiling because she's just served her husband 'his first cup of pure Brazilian coffee'. Before leaving for work, he has promised her new living room curtains, five bossa nova lessons, and another loan for her ne'er-do-well brother.

Coffee never made much of an impact in the UK during the first half of the 20th century. Tea remained the national drink, with the exception of a small number of London's cosmopolitans who associated espresso and cappuccino with being hip and cool. (They had their counterparts, of course, across the Atlantic.) The first London café with a Gaggia machine was Bar Moka, in Frith Street, Soho, which was opened by Gina Lollobrigida in 1953. Other bars opened in the area, which was heavily populated by Italian immigrants. But outside that enclave, what we would now identify as proper coffee remained a minority interest.

Drink and run: espresso being drunk, in a hurry, standing up, as soon as it comes from the machine in a Naples café. Al bar is the Italian phrase.

The second wave

By the mid-1960s, American coffee consumption had started to fall from its peak in the 1950s. Younger consumers increasingly preferred to get their caffeine from carbonated drinks, and coffee companies scrambled to find ways of convincing their customers of the superiority of their particular blend. And they had good reason to worry: most American coffee of the era, from large roasters, was pretty unmemorable stuff. But even as the mainstream was in decline, another development was taking place well under the radar of most of the coffee-drinking public.

In 1966, in the ever-innovative university city of Berkeley, California, a Dutch emigrant named Alfred Peet opened Peet's Coffee, a small shop selling beans for home brewing. Peet favoured a dark roast, perhaps similar to what his father had roasted in Europe. The shop inspired a keen local following, and five years later he began to supply three friends who wanted to open their own store in Seattle, Washington.

Peet's is still at its original address, and at well over 100 others in California and other states. The little shop in Seattle? It was called Starbucks. In 1984 Peet's was sold to a group of investors that included Jerry Baldwin, one of the three friends who started Starbucks. In 1987 the original three sold the Starbucks chain to an ex-employee named Howard Schultz, who had left the company to start up his own chain of coffee shops. It was Schultz who had the idea that Starbucks should emphasize brewed coffee rather than just sell beans. When he took over Starbucks, he put his plan into action on a large scale. In 1989, Starbucks had 46 branches in the Northwest and Midwest USA. At the time of writing, they have around 23,000 branches worldwide.

Starbucks is generally (and rightly) credited with playing a major role in this

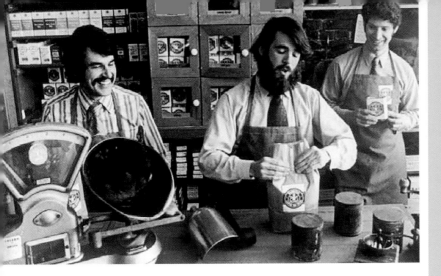

Facing page (left): Opening scene of a revolution in the bean: Alfred Peet serving customers at his Berkeley store in the late 1960s; (top right) Peet at the roaster. This is a very small roaster, entirely hand-operated; (bottom right) The original Peet's building at Walnut and Vine, Berkeley. Above: The founders of Starbucks in the early 1970s.

second wave of interest in coffee. The first wave had been concerned with increasing markets and delivering a consistent product to them – with quality a secondary consideration as long as it was perceived to be acceptable. Companies like Peet's showed that coffee could be better than that, and increased the demand for better beans and better brewing skills. But the second wave was also about coffee as part of a way of life: one lived in cafés and coffee shops and hip restaurants.

SINGLE-SERVE COFFEE

In 1986 the Nestlé corporation began selling Nespresso, a 'pod' of pre-measured coffee in a sealed capsule that could be used to brew a single cup of coffee. The product took over a decade to achieve market success – but once it did, it won big, and spawned a sizeable number of competitors: Tassimo, Senseo, and Keurig's K-Cup are just three of the most prominent.

We can see the attraction of single-serve systems. They're neat, they're consistent, and they eliminate the 'fear factor': when you're brewing your morning cup, you don't have to worry about whether the grind is right or the cafetière clean enough.

There are also plenty of arguments against single-serve. The coffee does not deliver outstanding quality in the cup. The cost is higher than for coffee made conventionally. While some systems consist of just a filter bag with the coffee inside, others are aluminium or plastic 'capsules' which often end up in landfill after their single use. And individual brands of capsule often have to be made in that manufacturer's own machines.

Single-serve coffee, for us, serves a similar purpose to that formerly served by instant. It is not the best way to enjoy coffee, but it can be the beginning of an individual's journey into coffee. Start with it, and if it gives you a taste for coffee, then it can lead to better things.

COFFEE IN THE 21ˢᵀ CENTURY

Since around the turn of the millennium there has been talk of a 'third wave' in coffee appreciation, and it is the one that we have been waiting for and want to promote. This wave is concerned pre-eminently with two things. One is quality: quality in the bean, in roasting and in the cup. The other is sourcing – going out to the producers and working with them to help them make their beans as good as they can be.

From good sourcing follow transparency and traceability: knowing exactly where the beans have come from, and through what commercial arrangements, and being able to pass on this information to consumers. We don't talk about regions, we talk about farms.

And we are not alone, needless to say. Long before the third wave of coffee began, independent roasters were springing up in Europe, the USA, Asia and the Antipodes. Our sector was (and is still) known as speciality coffee, and organizations were formed to pool our resources to share our collective expertise. The first group was the Specialty Coffee Association of America (SCAA), founded in 1982. Now there are groups all over the world, in both producing and consuming nations.

As of 2014, according to coffee-market specialists Allegra Strategies, the UK had around 16,500 coffee shops with revenues of over £6 billion, and they predicted continuing strong growth, with a forecast that the total UK coffee shop market would be more than 20,000 outlets with a turnover exceeding £8.5 billion by 2018. Just over half of this was accounted for by the three biggest chains (Starbucks, Costa and Caffè Nero), and the same general trends apply in the USA.

But the chains are not the only force in the marketplace. One of the great features of the third wave in coffee appreciation is the rising number of independent coffee shops. In London, where we live, something new seems to pop up every single day. Sometimes the shops are in central locations paying high rents, but many are in more out-of-the-way areas where rents are lower and they can afford to do things on a shoestring. These independents are not aiming to be the next Starbucks or Costa – or at least it doesn't seem that way. And sometimes they don't even need to create their own café, but set up in someone else's premises – bicycle repair shops are especially popular, and so are clothing stores. Often put together with random lots of paint and furniture, they're quite happy to look shabby as long as they get the coffee right. That's why they go into the business: for love of coffee. Just like us.

The big and the small

The small, quality-led companies in the speciality coffee sector represent a relatively small (though growing) percentage of the world market. Figures are hard to come by, but it is around 20 per cent in the USA and 10 per cent in Europe.

Far greater in size and commercial clout are the large traders and roasters, nearly all owned by huge multinationals, which control around half the global coffee market. They need vast quantities of coffee: to give an example, the largest companies may roast nearly 700,000 tonnes a year, as compared with our 500 tonnes a year. They have huge, complex trading operations to handle all their buying for them, and rarely (if ever) deal directly with farms. Nearly all their buying is done through middlemen in the producing countries, who buy and blend the green beans into large lots.

The ranking and market share (and ownership) of the top players in the industry change, but at the time of writing they include Kraft Foods (brands include Maxwell House), Nestlé (brands include Nescafé) and Procter & Gamble (brands include Folgers).

In response to consumer demand, the large traders and roasters have made efforts to engage with various certifying bodies, including Fairtrade and Rainforest Alliance. Because of their size, however, and the large quantities of beans they need to roast, their coffees can never have the individual local character of those from smaller roasters.

While the large companies will dominate the coffee market in terms of earnings and roasting volumes for the foreseeable future, the future has never looked brighter for the independent sector. Creative coffee-mad people throughout the world get hooked on the mysteries behind their cup, and want to pursue them. They open up cafés and coffee shops. They take to the internet and blog away – sometimes with amazing fanaticism and expertise. And some of them take the ultimate crazy decision: they become coffee roasters. These people are the future of coffee. We're with them all the way.

TOP 25 COFFEE-CONSUMING COUNTRIES

The figures show per capita consumption (2013) by weight of beans. This is much more accurate than any other method: measuring by number of cups would give a skewed result, since cup sizes vary greatly. If you notice the absence of the UK, it's because the UK is down at number 40, with a relatively puny 1.7kg per person per year.

- Finland 12.1kg
- Norway 9.1kg
- Austria 8.8kg
- Denmark 8.8kg
- Switzerland 8.3kg
- Sweden 7.4kg
- Germany 6.8kg
- Belgium 6.7kg
- Brazil 6.0kg
- Greece 5.9kg
- Netherlands 5.8kg
- Estonia 5.6kg
- Italy 5.6kg
- Croatia 5.4kg
- Slovenia 5.3kg
- France 5.3kg
- Portugal 4.8kg
- Cyprus 4.7kg
- Spain 4.5kg
- USA 4.4kg
- Lithuania 3.9kg
- Slovakia 3.6kg
- Czech Republic 3.6kg
- Japan 3.5kg
- Bulgaria 3.5kg

(Data derived from consumption and information on population, International Coffee Organization)

Q&A: the barista

Canny coffee drinkers know that they can learn a lot (and have a good time) from talking to an expert barista as he or she works behind the bar. We put some commonly asked questions to our resident barista.

Geoff Cliff grew up in Staffordshire, England. Before becoming a barista, he worked in retail and café management, in a small town called Oundle, in Northamptonshire.

What made you decide to be a barista, and when did you start?

During a working gap year in 2012, I got a job in a café-roastery in Surrey Hills, Sydney, Australia. There I was introduced to the world of speciality coffee and never looked back. I worked in Reuben Hills, a café/roaster/retailer, waiting tables and working at the brew bar. In 2013 I moved to London, and worked at Dose Espresso as head barista. Since 2014 I have worked at Union Hand-Roasted, on the coffee-training team.

Dose is one of London's most successful cafés, and always crowded. What are the special challenges of working in such a busy place?

The main challenge of working in a busy café environment, other than maintaining coffee quality among baristas, is finding a balance between being knowledgeable and arrogant.

Why did you move over to training?

I have always found it fun and rewarding to impart knowledge to passionate people.

What is it that you like best about the work?

I get to work in an area that I would also consider to be a hobby.

How much coffee do you make when you're not on the job?

Not much. I brew at home during days off with AeroPress, French press and V60.

Do you make espresso at home?

No, it would be a very expensive hobby. You get used to working with some very fine kit at Union – or any good café.

What qualities does a good barista need?

People skills, a calm demeanour and an immense attention to detail.

And what's a really bad quality?

Arrogance: looking down on those who aren't seen as being as knowledgeable and looking at coffee with a closed mind.

You have a complete beginner standing in front of you. Assuming eagerness and aptitude, how long will it take you to train them to the point where you'd be happy to let them make you an espresso?

Technically speaking, given the knowledge of how to create espresso, they should be able to do it after a few hours of dedicated training. But to comfortably problem-solve and troubleshoot on a busy shift, you need at least four to six months of experience.

When you walk into a coffee bar, what do you look for – both in machinery and in the baristas?

A manual machine, beans from a reputable roaster, and a smiling barista.

Is there any one point that you emphasize above all others when you're training people?

PASSION is required to develop. Passion, passion, passion.

Is there any one point that baristas seem to have trouble taking on board?

The importance of precise measurements. People are often shocked when we say half a gram of coffee will make a big difference, and two seconds here or there will change the taste of their espresso. A trainee who doesn't take this on board will say, 'that'll do', and wonder why the quality of their coffee is deteriorating.

People sometimes talk about needing to get the 'four Ms' of espresso right: *miscela* (blend), *macinazione* (grinding), *macchina* (machine) and *mano* (the hand of the barista). In your personal view, does one of the four Ms stand out in importance over the others?

All four need to work in tandem but, to me, *mano* would be first – the skilled hand of the barista. You can have the best of everything but a lack of passion and skill will stop the effectiveness of the other three. *Macchina*, the espresso machine, is the least important of all four. A beat-up old machine can make good coffee, although consistency is difficult to achieve; a good machine will help improve not just consistency but quality and efficiency. And there should definitely be a fifth – does the Italian word for water begin with M?

You meet a young person at a party and they say they want to be a barista. What advice do you give them?

Go and work in a busy café that is quality-focused; read coffee books; and make coffee at home.

SPECIALITY COFFEE DRINKS

There are dozens of coffee drinks that originated in one place but have achieved widespread fame. This is just a small selection from that vast field.

IRISH COFFEE

There are innumerable drinks in alcohol-consuming nations where the local spirit is served with strong coffee, sugar and whipped or poured cream. Irish coffee is the most famous. The cream should float on top of the sweetened, alcohol-laced coffee. An oft-quoted quip from a writer named Alex Levine states that Irish coffee is the only drink that provides all four essential food groups: alcohol, caffeine, sugar and fat.

VIETNAMESE COFFEE

When Vietnam was a French colony, the colonial population wanted coffee with milk – but there was no dairy industry to supply it. They came up with a drip-brewed drink that combined very strong coffee with sweetened condensed milk, and served it cold rather than hot. The result is very distinctive, and very sweet, but even people who normally don't take milk or sugar in their coffee may develop a fondness for it. It's a good way to finish a Vietnamese restaurant meal.

ESPRESSO MARTINI

This popular drink was invented in the 1980s by a prominent London bartender named Dick Bradsell, apparently in response to a request from a model who said she wanted something that 'will wake me up, then f**k me up.' The original recipe is still the best: two shots of vodka, one of freshly brewed espresso, half a shot of coffee liqueur and a quarter shot of simple syrup (made from equal parts of sugar and water). Put in a shaker, fill with ice, shake vigorously until the shaker is frosty-cold, then strain into a Martini glass. Garnish with a coffee bean.

SPICED COFFEE

In the Middle East and North Africa, coffee is sometimes brewed with a flavouring of spice. Cardamom is perhaps the most common, followed by cinnamon. The best coffee to use is one brewed small and strong, such as Turkish coffee.

AFFOGATO

Properly speaking, this is not a drink but a dessert. It consists of a scoop of vanilla ice cream, served in a bowl or glass, with a shot of espresso poured over. Sometimes a shot of liqueur, especially amaretto, will be poured over as well. Delicious but not the ideal way to start the day.

VIENNESE COFFEE

This should really be called Austrian coffee, because there are so many variations. Halfway between a dessert and a drink, it can be made with espresso or with strong brewed coffee and is topped with whipped cream. Milk may be added before the cream, and the cream can be flavoured and/or sprinkled with cocoa or cinnamon.

TURKISH COFFEE

This is one of the oldest brewed coffee drinks, and is served all over the Middle East and in Greece and other countries of eastern and southern Europe. Water, very finely ground coffee and (almost always) sugar are mixed in a small pot with a long handle, heated over a flame until boiling, then left to settle briefly before pouring into the cup or glass.

FAMOUS CAFÉS

SANT'EUSTACHIO ROME

Rome abounds in good coffee. The Antico Caffè Greco near the Spanish Steps may be the most famous for cultural and historical associations – it was founded in 1760 and has numbered artists including Richard Wagner and Lord Byron among its clientele – but coffee-loving locals and visitors often go to another famous spot, Sant'Eustachio (a short distance from the Parthenon). The signature coffee here is served sweet (ask for *amaro* if you don't want sugar) and with an enormous crema – how they make it is a closely guarded secret. They buy their beans directly from small cooperatives and roast them in the back of the café.

Piazza Sant'Eustachio 82, Rome

CAFFÈ FLORIAN VENICE

Florian offers what may well be the most expensive cups of coffee on earth. What do you get with your drink? The luxury of sitting down in the Piazza San Marco and watching the world go by, everyone from well-dressed Venetians to shorts- and flip-flop-wearing tourists snapping selfies for sending off to the folks back home in Tokyo, Sydney or Chicago. And one of the best views of the great Basilica San Marco, down at the other end of the piazza. And the knowledge that you're sitting in a little patch of history: Florian was founded in 1720, the same year that Canaletto painted one of his celebrated pictures of the Basilica. Reason enough to pay those frightening prices – at least once, anyway.

Piazza San Marco 57, Venice

LES DEUX MAGOTS PARIS

Les Deux Magots has been so famous for so long, you have to resign yourself to seeing plenty of tourists there. It's worth a visit just to watch the fashionable denizens of this chic *quartier* stroll by, and imagine what it was like when the café played host to Paul Verlaine, Picasso, Jean-Paul Sartre, Hemingway and other artistic and intellectual eminences from its opening in 1884. Most people like to sit outside but the lovely interior is the place to be if the weather's inclement.

6 place Saint-Germain-des-Prés, 75006 Paris

BAR ITALIA LONDON

There can be few Londoners who haven't at least heard of Bar Italia, or passed it while walking to eat or drink at one of Soho's innumerable bars and restaurants. This tiny place has distinctive signage that has remained virtually unchanged since the day it opened in 1949, right down to the famous clock hanging to the left of the door, and a tiny interior dominated by the bar, the machines, and a huge poster of the boxer Rocky Marciano, a gift from Marciano's widow. Bar Italia is one of the few surviving remnants of Soho's colourful past. This is reason enough to go here.

22 Frith Street, London W1D 4RF

CAFFÈ REGGIO NEW YORK

By American standards, Caffè Reggio is steeped in history. It was used as a location for *The Godfather Part II* (1974), for instance, and John F. Kennedy made a speech outside during his presidential campaign in 1959. Located in the heart of Greenwich Village, Reggio was founded in 1927 by Domenico Parisi and claims to have been the first place in the USA to serve cappuccino. Much of the décor is original, and there are Italian artworks and antiques dating back as far as the 17th century, but pride of place goes to the original espresso machine (1902).

119 MacDougal Street, New York, NY 10012

• Two doors down is the Café Wha?, another place with historical and cultural connections: Bob Dylan and Jimi Hendrix are just two of the eminent musicians to have performed there early in their careers.

Coffee and food

Breakfast is the obvious time of day when coffee hits the spot as a complement to both sweet and savoury food as well as providing the required caffeine hit. In the USA it's also OK at lunchtime in a roadside diner, with a club sandwich or a burger. But we rarely think of coffee as having flavour profiles that 'match' foods in the way that wine or (increasingly nowadays) craft beer does.

For pastries and chocolate, it's a no-brainer, but our increasingly time-pressured grazing style of eating suits coffee perfectly – a platter of meats and cheeses, some Middle Eastern snack foods, and a range of street-style foods all go really well with coffee. Here are a few of our favourite pairings based upon the way we roast our coffees. But note – we make no claim that this list covers all combos!

BAKED GOODS

Buttery croissants – plain, chocolate or almond – and Brazil coffees

Fruit Danish loves coffee from Guatemala, Panama, Tanzania

Cinnamon rolls and Sumatra, Ethiopia (Harrar region) or, for a real treat, Yemen Mocha

CHOCOLATE

These are very general ideas; more fun can be had with single-origin chocolate and coffee combinations.

Milk Colombia, Rwanda, El Salvador

Dark Peru, Sumatra, Yemen

Pralines Brazil

SAVOURY FOODS

Mildly spiced dishes Ethiopia Yirgacheffe, Burundi

Blue cheeses Sumatra, Yemen

Tangy cheeses Costa Rica, Kenya

Strongly spiced curries & chillies – beer!

Steven and Jeremy at the OROMIO Coffee Farmers Union dry mill, Addis Ababa, Ethiopia, in 2015.

GLOSSARY

This glossary was created to provide the coffee lover with a broad knowledge of coffee terms.

AFRICAN BED (RAISED BED) A method of open-air drying for post-harvest processing. The African bed is a wood frame stretcher on legs, with a suspended net mesh that holds coffee beans (wet parchment or whole cherry) above the ground. The advantages are the beans are less likely to be contaminated from dirt on the ground, and the mesh promotes air circulation below as well as above the beans. Raised beds may be protected from wet weather under plastic sheeting (also called a parabolic dryer).

ARABICA *Coffea arabica* is the species cultivated to produce 75 per cent of the world's commercial coffee. The plant is an evergreen perennial of the *Rubiaceae* family and is considered superior in flavour to the other main species, Robusta.

BLEND Roasted coffee that consists of a mixture of beans from different producers and origins. A blend should be created to produce original and complex flavour profiles, although often a blend is created with lower grade coffee to achieve a commercial price point.

BREW RATIO Relationship between the weight of ground coffee and the weight of water used for brewing.

BREWING TIME The length of time that water is in contact with ground coffee during brewing.

CEMENT PATIO A method of open-air drying. Wet parchment coffee beans (or whole coffee cherries) are spread out to dry on a cement patio. Depending on the weather, drying takes between four and 14 days. The disadvantages are that the coffee is exposed during wet weather conditions, it requires a lot of space and it requires labour as the beans need to be turned over frequently to promote even drying.

COFFEE BERRY BORER A small beetle that burrows into the coffee cherry and eats the coffee beans.

COFFEE CHERRY The common term for the fruit of the coffee tree. After flowering, the fruit takes about nine months to ripen. Each cherry normally contains two seeds, which we know as coffee beans. Ripe cherries can be red or yellow, sometimes orange. High-quality coffee requires cherries harvested at the peak of ripeness. With yellow varieties, it is more difficult to distinguish ripeness by colour.

COFFEE FLOWER *Coffea* is a genus of flowering plants and is a member of the family *Rubiaceae*. The coffee tree produces highly scented white flowers.

COFFEE WASHING STATION (CWS) The facility where freshly delivered coffee cherries from small-scale farmers are processed collectively and converted into parchment coffee. The term is used mainly in Africa: Rwanda, Kenya, Ethiopia and Burundi.

COFFEE WASTE WATER Sometimes called coffee effluent, this is what's left after using the washed process. Untreated coffee waste water is polluted with organic matter and is highly acidic. It has to be filtered and restored to neutral pH before being discharged into surface water. Semi-washed (pulped/honey) coffees produce less waste water than fully washed coffees. The natural (dry) process produces no waste water.

COMMODITY COFFEE The most basic quality level of coffee, sold at or near the base price set in either New York (Arabica) or Robusta (London). Commodity coffee has no intrinsic value related to its quality.

COOPERATIVE A group of small-scale farmers or organizations working together for the purpose of improving their businesses. They do things such as plan production levels, decide and enforce quality standards, promote new technologies, and help reduce production costs.

CREMA The head of caramel-coloured foam on the top of an espresso. It is created through extraction under pressure.

CUP OF EXCELLENCE A competition platform that began in 1999 as a way to improve quality and raise awareness of high-quality coffee in both producing and consuming countries. The programme evaluates and grades high-quality coffee from a particular country and sells the winning coffees through an international internet auction.

CUPPING The assessment of the quality of brewed coffee from aroma and taste. A standardized cupping protocol is used, for example the one created by the Specialty Coffee Association of America (SCAA).

DEFECT An imperfection in a bean that can cause a bad taste in the coffee. Often attributed to poor post-harvest processing.

DEMUCILAGINATOR Mechanical machines that scrub or squeeze the mucilage off the skinned beans. It is a modernization of the traditional 'ferment and wash' processing method (*see* Fermentation). In recent years, producers have started experimenting by removing varying amounts of the mucilage from the bean (*see* Honey process).

DEPULPING Removing the outer skin and some of the fruit pulp from the cherry.

DEPULPING MACHINE This removes the outer skin of the coffee cherry while leaving the mucilage in place.

DIALLING-IN The trade term for adjusting the espresso grinder to produce coarser or finer grinds until the extraction of the shot is correct and the coffee tastes good.

DRY MILL *See* Milling

DRY PROCESS *See* Natural process

ESTATE Sometimes called coffee plantations, these are large coffee farms, 50 hectares (120 acres) or more in size. They may be owned by a single family or by a company.

EXTRACTION This is what happens during brewing, when the soluble aroma and flavour compounds in the ground coffee dissolve in the water.

FAIRTRADE An international organization that certifies cooperatives and ensures that a minimum export price is guaranteed for their coffee.

FERMENTATION A stage of post-harvest processing in which the coffee pulp is softened, then washed off with water. The water needs to be refreshed two or three times until all the pulp is removed and the coffee is ready to dry.

GRADING *See* Screen size

GREEN BEAN A term for the unroasted coffee bean. Coffee is exported as green beans, normally in 60, 69 or 70kg sacks.

GREENHOUSE Plastic sheeting placed over drying coffee beans to protect them from weather conditions. The greenhouse should allow good air flow. It can be extremely hot within the greenhouse, which can cause the beans to dry too quickly, creating undesirable conditions for the workers who turn the beans to achieve even drying.

GRIND SIZE, OR PARTICLE SIZE The fineness of ground coffee, which must be suitable for the method of brewing.

HARD BEAN Term mainly used in Central America, referring to beans cultivated between 1200–1400m (4000–4500 ft) above sea level. Beans grown at higher altitudes mature more slowly, making them denser and giving higher sugar content and flavour.

HEIRLOOM VARIETIES Varieties of coffee that have been cultivated by tradition for many generations but often not documented.

HONEY PROCESS This is a processing method (called *miel* in Spanish) used by producers mostly in Central America. The skin of the coffee cherry is removed, leaving varying amounts of the pulpy mucilage on the beans' surface as they dry under controlled conditions. The process is called white, yellow, red or black honey, depending on the amount of the mucilage left on the bean.

HULLING *See* Milling

INTEGRATED PEST MANAGEMENT A pest control approach aimed at minimizing any harmful impact to people and the environment. Integrated practices minimize the use of fertilizers and pesticides, and partially and gradually replace them with organic fertilizers and biological disease control. The aim is to establish a balance between environmental protection and economic gain through permanent monitoring of parameters.

INTERNATIONAL COFFEE AGREEMENT A quota system agreed between producing and consuming countries where supplies of coffee in excess of consumer requirements are withheld from the market in order to stabilize prices and prevent swings in supply and demand. It is controlled by the International Coffee Organization.

LATTE ART Designs on the top of a caffè latte created by delicately pouring steamed and textured milk into the espresso.

LEAF RUST This is the fungus *Hemileia vastatrix*, which infects the coffee tree and creates rust-coloured spots on the leaves. Photosynthesis is halted, killing the plant.

LOT A quantity of coffee selected for particular reasons (such as quality) for processing and roasting separately.

MACHINE DRYING This technique is sometimes used to dry parchment coffee. The most common dryers are rotating drums that create a constant warm air flow that removes moisture. Firewood or coffee hull is often used as a heat source. The advantage over sun drying is that less space is required and it is not subject to weather conditions. The disadvantages are that driers can get too hot, which is detrimental to the beans, and wood smoke can contaminate the beans.

MEDIUM-SCALE FARMER A coffee producer with between 5 and 25 hectares (12–60 acres).

MICROFOAM Tiny bubbles created in milk during correct steaming to create a thick, viscous texture. *See* Latte art.

MICRO-LOT A small volume of coffee (typically 25 bags or less), processed and sold separately from a larger volume of production because it possesses a special character. Selection requires cupping small lots individually and making qualitative selection within an active relationship between farmer and buyer.

MILL(LING), DRY MILL Also called hulling. The process whereby parchment coffee is converted into green coffee beans: the parchment layer is removed by mechanical milling.

MOISTURE METER A machine used to measure the moisture content of dried coffee beans.

MONSOONED This refers to a processing technique in which harvested coffee beans are exposed to humid weather conditions to reduce their acidity. Used mainly in India's Malabar region.

MOUTHFEEL The physical sensation experienced when tasting brewed coffee. Mouthfeel is not about flavour but about texture, which can range from thin and light to heavy and syrupy.

MUCILAGE The thick, gluey flesh or pulp of the coffee cherry lying under the skin and surrounding the seeds.

NATURAL PROCESS Picked coffee cherries are laid out in the sun until the cherry is blackened and dried. Defective beans must be removed by hand. They're hulled once they are completely dry. This post-harvest processing method is often used in countries where rainfall is scarce and extended periods of sunshine are available to dry the coffee.

NEW CROP Green beans from the most recent harvest. These coffees are noted for their freshness.

ORGANIC COFFEE Coffee that has been cultivated and processed without the use of synthetic fertilizers or pesticides, and sometimes with additional agricultural requirements. Coffee labelled organic must be certified by a third-party agency. The cost of certification can be high, and many farmers follow organic principles without having their coffee certified as organic. Certain chemicals may be allowed in exceptional circumstances, and individual countries have one or more certifying organizations.

OVER-EXTRACTION Removing too much soluble material from the ground coffee during brewing, creating a cup that is unpleasant and bitter.

PARCHMENT The papery membrane surrounding the green bean. 'Parchment coffee' describes beans that have been processed but are still in this protective layer, which is removed by dry milling when the beans are prepared for export.

PEABERRY A normal coffee seed (bean) comprises two hemispherical halves that grow together in each fruit. When only one (round) seed develops, it's called a peaberry.

PULPED NATURAL A processing method that removes the skin of the coffee cherry but leaves the fruit pulp on the beans during drying on raised beds or patios. A term first used in Brazil. Similar to honey process.

RED HONEY Refers to a processing method used among some producers in Central America. Only the skin of the fruit is removed, leaving all of the mucilage (fruit pulp) on the beans during drying. The mucilage causes the beans to dry with a reddish colour. It is similar to semi-washed, a term used mainly in Brazil.

RESTING This can refer to two things. One: parchment coffee is stored for a time before milling and grading to allow moisture levels within the bean to even out. Two: coffee is rested (also called de-gassing) after roasting before being used to brew.

ROBUSTA *Coffea robusta* (or *Coffea canephora*) represents about a quarter of commercial coffee production. It is easier to grow at lower altitudes than Arabica and more resistant to disease, but is considered inferior in flavour.

SACK A jute, hessian or burlap bag used to transport green coffee. The weight depends on the country of origin. It's usually 60kg in Brazil, Africa, and Asia; 69kg in Central America and South America (except Brazil); and 70kg in Colombia. World export figures are quoted in 60kg bags, larger sizes being adjusted to the 60kg equivalent.

SCAA Specialty Coffee Association of America. The SCAE is its European counterpart.

SCREEN SIZE Coffee is generally graded according to the size of the beans. The beans are separated using a selection of screens, each with different sized holes.

SELECTIVE PICKING Making sure that only perfectly ripe cherries are harvested. Picking individual cherries by hand is labour-intensive and costly. But it is an important harvesting practice to produce high quality. Strip picking – removing the fruit from the whole branch at the same time, regardless of quality – is the contrary practice.

SEMI-WASHED *See* Pulped natural, Red honey

SILVERSKIN A delicate tissue ('paper') layer that adheres to the green bean, just under the parchment. It becomes free during roasting and is collected separately as a waste product called chaff. You shouldn't see any in your coffee beans, but occasionally small fragments escape the removal process.

SINGLE ORIGIN Refers to coffee grown in a specific geographical area, whether a region, a farm or a country.

SMALLHOLDER A small coffee producer, usually with less than 5 hectares (12 acres) of land – sometimes *much* less.

SOFT BEAN A term used mostly in Central America for beans cultivated below 1200m (4000ft) above sea level.

SPECIALITY COFFEE Coffee graded and traded on the basis of inherent quality, determined as 80 points or above in a 100-point scale created by the SCAA. Speciality coffees are distinctive because of their flavour and for having minimal (sometimes zero) defects.

STRICTLY HARD BEAN Term used mostly in Central America for beans cultivated above 1370m (4500ft) above sea level. The theory suggests that beans grown at higher altitudes mature more slowly, producing denser and sweeter (and thus preferable) beans.

STRIP PICKING A method of harvesting coffee by pickers who remove all the cherries from the branch at one time by running their hands down the branch. This dislodges unripe and over-ripe fruit too. Unless the cherries are hand-sorted later, cup quality will be affected.

SUN DRYING An ecologically sound way of drying coffee beans. However, it is a slow process (up to 14 days) and it needs a lot of space. Coffee is sun dried using various systems: cement patios, African beds, or greenhouses.

TAMPING Technique used in espresso brewing to pack down the ground coffee particles to form a flat tight bed.

TERROIR A characteristic flavour profile imparted to a coffee by the natural environment where it was produced, which includes the climate, soil and topography.

TRACEABLE/TRANSPARENT Providing detailed knowledge about a coffee lot so the identity is retained. Information relating to the production, location on the farm, date of harvesting, and prices paid to each participant throughout the coffee supply chain are all part of this.

UNION DIRECT TRADE The philosophy of our coffee sourcing. More than just paying a fair price, Union Direct Trade means we work in partnership with farmers to improve quality of coffee, and livelihoods, long term.

WASHED PROCESS *See* Wet process

WET MILL Coffee cherries are processed here into parchment coffee. In Latin America this is often called *beneficio humedo*; in Africa, Coffee Washing Station.

WET PROCESS A post-harvest process in which the skin of the coffee cherry and some of the pulp is detached by a depulping machine. The remaining pulp is removed by fermentation in tanks for around 24 hours (depending upon weather and temperature). The beans are washed with large amounts of water to produce clean, wet parchment coffee. This is then dried in the sun on large cement patios or on raised African beds.

RESOURCES

BOOKS

Allen, Stewart Lee *The Devil's Cup: Coffee, the Driving Force in History* (Canongate)

Digum, Gregory, and Nina Luttinger *The Coffee Book: Anatomy of an Industry from Crop to the Last Drop* (New Press)

Ellis, Markman *The Coffee-House: A Cultural History* (Weidenfeld & Nicolson)

Pendergrast, Mark *Uncommon Grounds: The History of Coffee and How It Transformed Our World* (Basic Books)

Viani, Rinantonio and Andrea Illy (Eds) *Espresso Coffee: The Science of Quality* (Academic Press)

Wild, Antony *Black Gold: The Dark History of Coffee* (Harper)

WEBSITES

There are some excellent coffee websites out there, though some of the good ones do not get updated often. Where the subject is coffee history, this doesn't matter. For other subjects, pay attention to the copyright line: this will tell you when the site was last updated.

Australian Specialty Coffee Association
www.australianspecialtycoffee.com.au

Caffeine Magazine
www.caffeinemag.com
A bimonthly magazine published in London.

www.coffeegeek.com
Not the easiest site to navigate, but it has a lot of information. Especially good if you're looking for advice on equipment or technique.

Coffee Chemistry
www.coffeechemistry.com
Technical but interesting.

Coffee Forums
www.coffeeforums.com
www.coffeeforums.co.uk

Coffee Research
www.coffeeresearch.org

Counterculture
counterculturecoffee.com
A US-based roaster and retailer that also offers training at regional centres.

Ethical Trading Initiative
www.ethicaltrade.org

www.ineedcoffee.com
A pleasure to use and offering hours of well-informed reading on history, technique, travel and many other topics.

International Coffee Organization
www.ico.org

www.jimseven.com
The blog published by James Hoffman, co-founder of Square Mile Coffee.

New Zealand Specialty Coffee Association
www.nzcra.org.nz

Perfect Daily Grind
www.perfectdailygrind.com
A website and blog devoted to the speciality coffee industry.

Quality Coffee Institute
www.coffeeinstitute.org

Speciality Coffee Association of America
www.scaa.org

Speciality Coffee Association of Europe

www.scae.com

Union Hand-Roasted Coffee

www.unionroasted.com

World Coffee Research

worldcoffeeresearch.org

COFFEE FESTIVALS

Growing in popularity, festivals are good places for tasting, buying, and watching demonstrations and talks. Here are just a few of the most prominent. Note that on some days, these festivals tend to be open only to people in the industry.

Amsterdam

amsterdamcoffeefestival.com

London

www.londoncoffeefestival.com

Melbourne

www.internationalcoffeeexpo.com

New York

www.newyorkcoffeefestival.com

San Francisco, Los Angeles and Chicago

www.coffee-con.com

Above: Picking coffee at Finca Emporium, Boquete, Panama.
Centre: Ben concentrating on a micro-lot roast in our small batch roastery.
Bottom: From field to cup. The coffee finally ready to taste.

INDEX

Page numbers in **bold** refer to feature boxes. Page numbers in *italics* refer to illustration captions.

AUTHOR ACKNOWLEDGEMENTS

Of course we have to thank our parents. They may have thought we were insane when we chucked in our professional careers and started roasting coffee, but they always gave us unconditional love, support and a roof over our heads.

We'd be nowhere without our outstanding team at Union who've helped us build the company, sharing our ethos of fabulous-tasting coffee underpinned by ethical trading. Special thanks to Pascale Schuit, who has brought an intellectual insight into developing our concept of Union Direct Trade, and her thinking, writing and photographs are included in this book.

From the early days, the synchronicity of meeting Scott and Ally Svensen accelerated us on a path we could never have predicted. John and Philip Schluter have been steady counsellors as we picked our way through understanding the coffee supply chain. We also appreciate Dr Aaron Davis (Royal Botanic Gardens, Kew) for work on coffee and climate change.

Our relationship with Rwanda has been formative in enabling us to understand our obligation to achieve sustainable trade, and for this we thank Tim Schilling, Paul DeLucco, Tom Bagaza, Pascale Kalisa and Zacharie Ntakirutimana.

We also give big thanks to our editor, Richard Ehrlich (who first wrote about us back in our infancy coffee days and has followed our progress steadily), for his excellent technique in distilling our opinions into coherent copy. And to Fiona Holman, editorial director, for her energy, determination and enthusiasm. And finally to Maggie Ramsay, who not only copy-edited our manuscript with consummate skill but discovered her inner coffee-geek in the process.

PICTURE CREDITS

Advertising Archives pages 29, 150 above left
Bezzera page 130 below
Bridgeman Images pages 79, 129 above left, 148, 150 above right, 160 below
Corbis pages 2, 42, 149 left, 151, 158 centre and right, 159, 160 centre, 162
Counter Culture Coffee flavor wheel page 93
Stephen Cummiskey pages 46, 47
Getty Images pages 129 above right, 130 above, 131 above, 150 below
Lee Hall 102 below
Haraala Hamilton: front cover, pages 3–4, 7, 73, 75, 76, 77, 78, 80, 81, 82, 84, 88, 89, 94. 95, 98, 99, 100, 102 above, 104, 105, 1-6, 107, 108, 109, 111, 112, 113 below, 115, 117, 119, 121, 123, 125, 133, 134, 135, 139, 140, 141, 142, 143, 144, 145, 157, 169 centre and below, 176
La Marzocco page 131
Mary Evans Picture Library page 16, 129 below, 149 right
Jonathan Pearmain pages 11, 18
Peet's page 152
SCAA page 96
Stockfood page 158 left
Union Hand-Roasted Coffee pages 10, 11, 14, 15, 17, 18, 19, 21, 22, 23, 24, 25, 26, 27, 30, 34, 36, 39, 41, 44, 48, 50, 51, 53, 54, 56. 57. 58, 59, 60, 61, 63, 64, 65, 67, 68, 69, 97, 101, 102 below, 113 above, 128 above, 131, 156, 163, 169 above

First published in 2016 in the United Kingdom by
Pavilion
43 Great Ormond Street
London WC1N 3HZ

Copyright © 2016 Pavilion Books Company Ltd
Text copyright © 2016 Union Hand-Roasted Coffee

This book can be ordered direct from the publisher at
www.pavilionbooks.com

ISBN 978-1-910-49632-9

A CIP catalogue record for this book is available from the British Library.

10 9 8 7 6 5 4 3 2

Reproduction by Mission Productions Ltd, Hong Kong
Printed and bound by Toppan Leefung Printing Ltd, China